Switzerland

Jacques Casanova de Seingalt

[ZHINGOORA BOOKS]

THE ETERNAL QUEST

SWITZERLAND

CHAPTER XIII

I Resolve to Become a Monk—I go to Confession—Delay of a Fortnight—Giustiniani, the Apostle Capuchin—I Alter my Mind; My Reasons—My Pranks at the Inn—I Dine With the Abbot

The cool way in which the abbot told these cock-and-bull stories gave me an inclination to laughter, which the holiness of the place and the laws of politeness had much difficulty in restraining. All the same I listened with such an attentive air that his reverence was delighted with me and asked where I was staying.

"Nowhere," said I; "I came from Zurich on foot, and my first visit was to your church."

I do not know whether I pronounced these words with an air of compunction, but the abbot joined his hands and lifted them to heaven, as if to thank God for touching my heart and bringing me there to lay down the burden of my sins. I have no doubt that these were his thoughts, as I have always had the look of a great sinner.

The abbot said it was near noon and that he hoped I would do him the honour of dining with him, and I accepted with pleasure, for I had had nothing to eat and I knew that there is usually good cheer in such places. I did not know where I was and I did not care to ask, being willing to leave him under the impression that I was a pilgrim come to expiate my sins.

On our way from the church the abbot told me that his monks were fasting, but that we should eat meat in virtue of a dispensation he had received from Benedict XIV., which allowed him to eat meat all the year round with his guests. I replied that I would join him all the more willingly as the Holy Father had given me a similar dispensation. This seemed to excite his curiosity about myself, and when we got to his room, which did not look the cell of a penitent, he hastened to shew me the brief, which he had framed and glazed and hung up opposite the table so that the curious and scrupulous might have it in full view.

As the table was only laid for two, a servant in full livery came in and brought another cover; and the humble abbot then told me that he usually had his chancellor with him at dinner, "for," said he, "I have a chancery, since as abbot of Our Lady of Einsiedel I am a prince of the Holy Roman Empire."

This was a relief to me, as I now knew where I was, and I no longer ran the risk of shewing my ignorance in the course of conversation.

This monastery (of which I had heard before) was the Loretto of the Mountains, and was famous for the number of pilgrims who resorted to it.

In the course of dinner the prince—abbot asked me where I came from, if I were married, if I intended to make a tour of Switzerland, adding that he should be glad to give me letters of introduction. I replied that I was a Venetian, a bachelor, and that I should be glad to accept the letters of introduction he had kindly offered me, after I had had a private conference with him, in which I desired to take his advice on my conscience.

Thus, without premeditation, and scarcely knowing what I was saying, I engaged to confess to the abbot.

This was my way. Whenever I obeyed a spontaneous impulse, whenever I did anything of a sudden, I thought I was following the laws of my destiny, and yielding to a supreme will. When I had thus plainly intimated to him that he was to be my confessor, he felt obliged to speak with religious fervour, and his discourses seemed tolerable enough during a delicate and appetising repast, for we had snipe and woodcock; which made me exclaim,—

"What! game like that at this time of year?"

"It's a secret," said he, with a pleased smile, "which I shall be glad to communicate to you."

The abbot was a man of taste, for though he affected sobriety he had the choicest wines and the most delicious dishes on the table. A splendid salmon-trout was brought, which made him smile with pleasure, and seasoning the good fare with a jest, he said in Latin that we must taste it as it was fish, and that it was right to fast a little.

While he was talking the abbot kept a keen eye on me, and as my fine dress made him feel certain that I had nothing to ask of him he spoke at ease.

When dinner was over the chancellor bowed respectfully and went out. Soon after the abbot took me over the monastery, including the library, which contained a portrait of the Elector of Cologne in semi-ecclesiastical costume. I told him that the portrait was a good though ugly likeness, and drew out of my pocket the gold snuffbox the prince had given me, telling him that it was a speaking likeness. He looked at it with interest, and thought his highness had done well to be taken in the dress of a grand-master. But I perceived that the elegance of the snuff-box did no harm to the opinion the abbot had conceived of me. As for the library, if I had been alone it would have made me weep. It contained nothing under the size of folio, the newest books were a hundred years old, and the subject-matter of all these huge books was solely theology and controversy. There were Bibles, commentators, the Fathers, works on canon law in German, volumes of annals, and Hoffman's dictionary.

"I suppose your monks have private libraries of their own," I said, "which contain accounts of travels, with historical and scientific works."

"Not at all," he replied; "my monks are honest folk, who are content to do their duty, and to live in peace and sweet ignorance."

I do not know what happened to me at that moment, but a strange whim came into my head—I would be a monk, too. I said nothing about it at the moment, but I begged the abbot to take me to his private chamber.

"I wish to make a general confession of all my sins," said I, "that I may obtain the benefit of absolution, and receive the Holy Eucharist on the morrow."

He made no answer, but led the way to a pretty little room, and without requiring me to kneel down said he was ready to hear me.

I sat down before him and for three consecutive hours I narrated scandalous histories unnumerable, which, however, I told simply and not spicily, since I felt ascetically disposed and obliged myself to speak with a contrition I did not feel, for when I recounted my follies I was very far from finding the remembrance of them disagreeable.

In spite of that, the serene or reverend abbot believed, at all events, in my attrition, for he told me that since by the appointed means I had once more placed myself in a state of grace, contrition would be perfected in me.

According to the good abbot, and still more according to me, without grace contrition is impossible.

After he had pronounced the sacramental words which take away the sins of men, he advised me to retire to the chamber he had appointed for me, to pass the rest of the day in prayer, and to go to bed at an early hour, but he added that I could have supper if I was accustomed to that meal. He told me that I might communicate at the first mass next morning, and with that we parted.

I obeyed with a docility which has puzzled me ever since, but at the time I thought nothing of it. I was left alone in a room which I did not even examine, and there I pondered over the idea which had come into my head before making my confession; and I quite made up my mind that chance, or rather my good genius, had led me to that spot, where happiness awaited me, and where I might shelter all my days from the tempests of the world.

"Whether I stay here," said I, "depends on myself alone, as I am sure the abbot will not refuse me the cowl if I give him ten thousand crowns for my support."

All that was needed to secure my happiness seemed a library of my own choosing, and I did not doubt but that the abbot would let me have what books I pleased if I promised to leave them to the monastery after my death.

As to the society of the monks, the discord, envy, and all the bickerings inseparable from such a mode of life, I thought I had nothing to pass in that way, since I had no ambitions which could rouse the jealousy of the other monks. Nevertheless, despite my fascination, I foresaw the possibility of repentance, and I shuddered at the thought, but I had a cure for that also.

"When I ask for the habit," I said, "I will also ask that my novitiate be extended for ten years, and if repentance do not come in ten years it will not come at all. I shall declare that I do not wish for any cure or any ecclesiastical dignity. All I want is peace and leave to follow my own tastes, without scandalising anyone." I thought: I could easily remove any objections which might be made to the long term of my novitiate, by agreeing, in case I changed my mind, to forfeit the ten thousand crowns which I would pay in advance.

I put down this fine idea in writing before I went to bed; and in the morning, finding myself unshaken in my resolve, after I had communicated I gave my plan to the abbot, who was taking chocolate in his room.

He immediately read my plan, and without saying anything put it on the table, and after breakfast he walked up and down the room and read it again, and finally told me that he would give me an answer after dinner.

I waited till night with the impatience of a child who has been promised toys on its birthday—so completely and suddenly can an infatuation change one's nature. We had as good a dinner as on the day before, and when we had risen from the table the good abbot said,

"My carriage is at the door to take you to Zurich. Go, and let me have a fortnight to think it over. I will bring my answer in person. In the meanwhile here are two sealed letters, which please deliver yourself."

I replied that I would obey his instructions and that I would wait for him at the "Sword," in the hope that he would deign to grant my wishes. I took his hand, which he allowed me to kiss, and I then set out for Zurich.

As soon as my Spaniard saw me the rascal began to laugh. I guessed what he was thinking, and asked him what he was laughing at.

"I am amazed to see that no sooner do you arrive in Switzerland than you contrive to find some amusement which keeps you away for two whole days."

"Ah, I see; go and tell the landlord that I shall want the use of a good carriage for the next fortnight, and also a guide on whom I can rely."

My landlord, whose name was Ote, had been a captain, and was thought a great deal of at Zurich. He told me that all the carriages in the neighbourhood were uncovered. I said they would do, as there was nothing better to be had, and he informed me I could trust the servant he would provide me with.

Next morning I took the abbot's letters. One was for M. Orelli and the other for a M. Pestalozzi, neither of whom I found at home; but in the afternoon they both called on me, asked me to dinner, and made me promise to come with them the same evening to a concert. This is the only species of entertainment allowed at Zurich, and only members of the musical society can be present, with the exception of strangers, who have to be introduced by a member, and are then admitted on the payment of a crown. The two gentlemen both spoke in very high terms of the Abbot of Einsiedel.

I thought the concert a bad one, and got bored at it. The men sat on the right hand and the women on the left. I was vexed with this arrangement, for in spite of my recent conversation I saw three or four ladies who pleased me, and whose eyes wandered a good deal in my direction. I should have liked to make love to them, to make the best of my time before I became a monk.

When the concert was over, men and women went out together, and the two citizens presented me to their wives and daughters, who looked pleasant, and were amongst those I had noticed.

Courtesy is necessarily cut short in the street, and, after I had thanked the two gentlemen, I went home to the "Sword."

Next day I dined with M. Orelli, and I had an opportunity for doing justice to his daughter's amiability without being able to let her perceive how she had impressed me. The day after, I played the same part with M. Pestalozzi, although his charming daughter was pretty enough to excite my gallantry. But to my own great astonishment I was a mirror of discretion, and in four days that was my character all over the town. I was quite astonished to find myself accosted in quite a respectful manner, to which I was not accustomed; but in the pious state of mind I was in, this confirmed me in the belief that my idea of taking the cowl had been a Divine inspiration. Nevertheless, I felt listless and weary, but I looked upon that as the inevitable consequence of so complete a change of life, and thought it would disappear when I grew more accustomed to goodness.

In order to put myself, as soon as possible, on an equality with my future brethren, I passed three hours every morning in learning German. My master was an extraordinary man, a native of Genoa, and an apostate Capuchin. His name was Giustiniani. The poor man, to whom I gave six francs every morning, looked upon me as an angel from heaven, although I, with the enthusiasm of a devotee, took him for a devil of hell, for he lost no opportunity of throwing a stone at the religious orders. Those orders which had the highest reputation, were, according to him, the worst of all, since they led more people astray. He styled monks in general as a vile rabble, the curse of the human race.

"But," said I to him one day, "you will confess that Our Lady of Einsiedel . . ."

"What!" replied the Genoese, without letting me finish my remark, "do you think I should make an exception in favour of a set of forty ignorant, lazy, vicious, idle, hypocritical scoundrels who live bad lives under the cloak of humility, and eat up the houses of the poor simpletons who provide for them, when they ought to be earning their own bread?"

"But how about his reverend highness the abbot?"

"A stuck-up peasant who plays the part of a prince, and is fool enough to think himself one."

"But he is a prince."

"As much a prince as I am. I look upon him as a mere buffoon."

"What has he done to you?"

"Nothing; but he is a monk."

"He is a friend of mine."

"I cannot retract what I have said, but I beg your pardon."

This Giustiniani had a great influence upon me, although I did not know it, for I thought my vocation was sure. But my idea of becoming a monk at Einsiedel came to an end as follows:

The day before the abbot was coming to see me, at about six o'clock in the evening, I was sitting at my window, which looked out on the bridge, and gazing at the passers-by, when all at once a carriage and four came up at a good pace and stopped at the inn. There was no footman on it, and consequently the waiter came out and opened the door, and I saw four well-dressed women leave the carriage. In the first three I saw nothing noticeable, but the fourth, who was dressed in a riding-habit, struck me at once with her elegance and beauty. She was a brunette with fine and well-set eyes, arched eyebrows, and a complexion in which the hues of the lily and the rose were mingled. Her bonnet was of blue satin with a silver fillet, which gave her an air I could not resist. I stretched out from the window as far as I could, and she lifted her eyes and looked at me as if I had bade her do so. My position obliged me to look at her for half a minute; too much for a modest woman, and more than was required to set me all ablaze.

I ran and took up my position at the window of my ante-chamber, which commanded a view of the staircase, and before long I saw her running by to rejoin her three companions. When she got opposite to my window she chanced to turn in that direction, and on seeing me cried out as if she had seen a ghost; but she soon recollected herself and ran away, laughing like a madcap, and rejoined the other ladies who were already in their room.

Reader, put yourself in my place, and tell me how I could have avoided this meeting. And you who would bury yourselves in monastic shades, persevere, if you can, after you have seen what I saw at Zurich on April 23rd.

I was in such a state of excitement that I had to lie down on my bed. After resting a few minutes, I got up and almost unconsciously went towards the passage window and saw the waiter coming out of the ladies' room.

"Waiter," said I, "I will take supper in the dining-room with everybody else."

"If you want to see those ladies, that won't do, as they have ordered their supper to be brought up to them. They want to go to bed in good time as they are to leave at day-break."

"Where are they going?"

"To Our Lady of Einsiedel to pay their vows."

"Where do they come from?"

"From Soleure."

"What are their names?"

"I don't know."

I went to lie down again, and thought how I could approach the fair one of my thoughts. Should I go to Einsiedel, too? But what could I do when I got there? These ladies are going to make their confessions; I could not get into the confessional. What kind of a figure should I cut among the monks? And if I were to meet the abbot on the way, how could I help returning with him? If I had had a trusty friend I would have arranged an ambuscade and carried off my charmer. It would have been an easy task, as she had nobody to defend her. What if I were to pluck up my heart and beg them to let me sup in their company? I was afraid of the three devotees; I should meet with a refusal. I judged that my charmer's devotion was more a matter of form than any thing else, as her physiognomy declared her to be a lover of pleasure, and I had long been accustomed to read womens' characters by the play of their features.

I did not know which way to turn, when a happy idea came into my head. I went to the passage window and stayed there till the waiter went by. I had him into the room, and began my discourse by sliding a piece of gold into his hand. I then asked him to lend me his green apron, as I wished to wait upon the ladies at supper.

"What are you laughing at?"

"At your taking such a fancy, sir, though I think I know why."

"You are a sharp fellow."

"Yes, sir, as sharp as most of them; I will get you a new apron. The pretty one asked me who you were."

"What did you tell her?"

"I said you were an Italian; that's all."

"If you will hold your tongue I will double that piece of gold."

"I have asked your Spaniard to help me, sir, as I am single-handed, and supper has to be served at the same time both upstairs and downstairs."

"Very good; but the rascal mustn't come into the room or he would be sure to laugh. Let him go to the kitchen, bring up the dishes, and leave them outside the door."

The waiter went out, and returned soon after with the apron and Le Duc, to whom I explained in all seriousness what he had to do. He laughed like a madman, but assured me he would follow my directions. I procured a carving-knife, tied my hair in a queue, took off my coat, and put on the apron over my scarlet waistcoat ornamented with gold lace. I then looked at myself in the glass, and thought my appearance mean enough for the modest part I was about to play. I was delighted at the prospect, and thought to myself that as the ladies came from Soleure they would speak French.

Le Duc came to tell me that the waiter was going upstairs. I went into the ladies' room and said, "Supper is about to be served, ladies."

"Make haste about it, then," said the ugliest of them, "as we have got to rise before day-break."

I placed the chairs round the table and glanced at my fair one, who looked petrified. The waiter came in, and I helped him to put the dishes on the table, and he then said to me, "Do you stay here, as I have to go downstairs."

I took a plate and stood behind a chair facing the lady, and without appearing to look at her I saw her perfectly, or rather I saw nothing else. She was astonished the others did not give me a glance, and they could not have pleased me better. After the soup I hurried to change her plate, and then did the same office for the rest: they helped themselves to the boiled beef.

While they were eating, I took a boiled capon and cut it up in a masterly manner.

"We have a waiter who knows his work," said the lady of my thoughts.

"Have you been long at this inn?"

"Only a few weeks, madam."

"You wait very well."

"Madam is very good."

I had tucked in my superb ruffles of English point lace, but my frilled shirt front of the same material protruded slightly through my vest, which I had not buttoned carefully. She saw it, and said, "Come here a moment."

"What does madam require?"

"Let me see it. What beautiful lace!"

"So I have been told, madam, but it is very old. An Italian gentleman who was staying here made me a present of it."

"You have ruffles of the same kind, I suppose?"

"Yes, madam;" and so saying I stretched out my hand, unbuttoning my waistcoat. She gently drew out the ruffle, and seemed to place herself in a position to intoxicate me with the sight of her charms, although she was tightly laced. What an ecstatic moment! I knew she had recognized me, and the thought that I could not carry the masquerade beyond a certain point was a veritable torment to me.

When she had looked a long time, one of the others said,

"You are certainly very curious, my dear, one would think you had never seen lace before."

At this she blushed.

When the supper was done, the three ugly ladies each went apart to undress, while I took away the dishes, and my heroine began to write. I confess that I was almost infatuated enough to think that she was writing to me; however, I had too high an opinion of her to entertain the idea.

As soon as I had taken away the dishes, I stood by the door in the respectful manner becoming the occasion.

"What are you waiting for?" she said.

"For your orders, madam."

"Thank you, I don't want anything."

"Your boots, madam, you will like them removed before you retire."

"True, but still I don't like to give you so much trouble."

"I am here to attend on you, madam."

So saying, I knelt on one knee before her, and slowly unplaced her boots while she continued writing. I went farther; I unbuckled her garters, delighting in the contemplation and still more in the touch of her delicately-shaped legs, but too soon for me she turned her head, and said,

"That will do, thank you. I did not notice that you were giving yourself so much trouble. We shall see you to-morrow evening."

"Then you will sup here, ladies?"

"Certainly."

I took her boots away, and asked if I should lock the door.

"No, my good fellow," said she, in the voice of a syren, "leave the key inside."

Le Duc took the charmer's boots from me, and said, laughing,—

"She has caught you."

"What?"

"I saw it all, sir, you played your part as well as any actor in Paris; and I am certain that she will give you a louis to-morrow, but if you don't hand it over to me I will blow on the whole thing."

"That's enough, you rascal; get me my supper as quickly as possible."

Such are the pleasures which old age no longer allows me to enjoy, except in my memory. There are monsters who preach repentance, and philosophers who treat all pleasures as vanity. Let them talk on. Repentance only befits crimes, and pleasures are realities, though all too fleeting.

A happy dream made me pass the night with the fair lady; doubtless it was a delusion, but a delusion full of bliss. What would I not give now for such dreams, which made my nights so sweet!

Next morning at day-break I was at her door with her boots in my hand just as their coachman came to call them. I asked them, as a matter of form, if they would have breakfast, and they replied merrily that they had made too good a supper to have any appetite at such an early hour. I went out of the room to give them time to dress, but the door was half open, and I saw reflected in the glass the snow-white bosom of my fair one; it was an intoxicating sight. When she had laced herself and put on her dress she called for her boots. I asked if I should put them on, to which she consented with a good grace, and as she had green velvet breeches, she seemed to consider herself as almost a man. And, after all, a waiter is not worth putting one's self out about. All the worst for him if he dare conceive any hopes from the trifling concessions he receives. His punishment will be severe, for who would have thought he could have presumed so far? As for me, I am now, sad to say, grown old, and enjoy some few privileges of this description, which I relish, though despising myself, and still more those who thus indulge me.

After she had gone I went to sleep again, hoping to see her in the evening. When I awoke I heard that the abbot of Einsiedel was at

Zurich, and my landlord told me that his reverend highness would dine with me in my room. I told him that I wished to treat the abbot well, and that he must set the best dinner he could for us.

At noon the worthy prelate was shewn up to my room, and began by complimenting me on the good reputation I had at Zurich, saying that this made him believe that my vocation was a real one.

"The following distich," he added, "should now become your motto:

"Inveni portum. Spes et fortuna valete;
Nil mihi vobiscum est: ludite nuns alios."

"That is a translation of two verses from Euripides," I answered; "but, my lord, they will not serve me, as I have changed my mind since yesterday."

"I congratulate you," said he, "and I hope you will accomplish all your desires. I may tell you confidentially that it is much easier to save one's soul in the world where one can do good to one's neighbours, than in the convent, where a man does no good to himself nor to anyone else."

This was not speaking like the hypocrite Guistiniani had described to me; on the contrary, it was the language of a good and sensible man.

We had a princely dinner, as my landlord had made each of the three courses a work of art. The repast was enlivened by an interesting conversation, to which wit and humour were not lacking. After coffee I thanked the abbot with the greatest respect, and accompanied him to his carriage, where the reverend father reiterated his offers of serving me, and thus, well pleased with one another, we parted.

The presence and the conversation of this worthy priest had not for a moment distracted my thoughts from the pleasing object with which they were occupied. So soon as the abbot had gone, I went to the bridge to await the blessed angel, who seemed to have been sent from Soleure with the express purpose of delivering me from the temptation to become a monk, which the devil had put into my heart. Standing on the bridge I built many a fine castle in Spain, and about six in the evening I had the pleasure of seeing my fair traveller once more. I hid myself so as to see without being seen. I was greatly surprised to see them all four looking towards my window. Their curiosity shewed me that the lady had told them of the secret, and with my astonishment there was some admixture of anger. This was only natural, as I not only saw myself deprived of the hope of making any further advances, but I felt that I could no longer play my part of waiter with any confidence. In spite of my love for the lady I would not for the world become the laughing-stock of her three plain companions. If I had interested her in my favour, she would certainly not have divulged my secret, and I saw in her doing so proof positive that she did not want the jest to go any further, or rather of her want of that spirit so necessary to ensure the success of an intrigue. If the three companions of my charmer had had anything attractive about them, I might possibly have persevered and defied misfortune; but in the same measure as beauty cheers my heart, ugliness depresses it. Anticipating the melancholy which I foresaw would result from this disappointment, I went out with the idea of amusing myself, and happening to meet Giustiniani I told him of my misfortune, saying that I should not be sorry to make up for it by a couple of hours of the society of some mercenary beauty.

"I will take you to a house," said he, "where you will find what you want. Go up to the second floor and you will be well received by an old woman, if you whisper my name to her. I dare not accompany you, as I am well known in the town and it might get me into trouble with the police, who are ridiculously strict in these matters. Indeed I advise you to take care that nobody sees you going in."

I followed the ex-Capuchin's advice and waited for the dusk of the evening. I had a good reception, but the supper was poor, and the hours that I spent with two young girls of the working class were tedious. They were pretty enough, but my head was full of my perfidious charmer, and besides, despite their neatness and prettiness, they were wanting in that grace which adds so many charms to pleasure. The liberality of my payment, to which they were not accustomed, captivated the old woman, who said she would get me all the best stuff in the town; but she warned me to take care that nobody saw me going into her house.

When I got back Le Duc told me that I had been wise to slip away, as my masquerade had become generally known, and the whole house, including the landlord, had been eagerly waiting to see me play the part of waiter. "I took your place," he added. "The lady who has taken your fancy is Madame——, and I must confess she is vastly fine."

"Did she ask where the other waiter was?"

"No, but the other ladies asked what had become of you several times."

"And Madame said nothing?"

"She didn't open her mouth, but looked sad and seemed to care for nothing, till I said you were away because you were ill."

"That was stupid of you. Why did you say that?"

"I had to say something."

"True. Did you untie her shoe?"

"No; she did not want me to do so."

"Good. Who told you her name?"

"Her coachman. She is just married to a man older than herself."

I went to bed, but could only think of the indiscretion and sadness of my fair lady. I could not reconcile the two traits in her character. Next day, knowing that she would be starting early, I posted myself at the window to see her get into the carriage, but I took care to arrange the curtain in such a way that I could not be seen. Madame was the last to get in, and pretending that she wanted to see if it rained, she took off her bonnet and lifted her head. Drawing the curtain with one hand, and taking off my cap with the other, I wafted her a kiss with the tips of my fingers. In her turn she bowed graciously, returning my kiss with a good-natured smile.

CHAPTER XIV

I Leave Zurich—Comic Adventure at Baden—Soleure—M. De Chavigni—M. and Madame * * * I Act in a Play—I Counterfeit Sickness to Attain Happiness

M. Mote, my landlord, introduced his two sons to me. He had brought them up like young princes. In Switzerland, an innkeeper is not always a man of no account. There are many who are as much respected as people of far higher rank are in other countries. But each country has its own manners. My landlord did the honours of the table, and thought it no degradation to make his guests pay for the meal. He was right; the only really degrading thing in the world is vice. A Swiss landlord only takes the chief place at table to see that everyone is properly attended to. If he have a son, he does not sit down with his father, but waits on the guests, with napkin in hand. At Schaffhaus, my landlord's son, who was a captain in the Imperial army, stood behind my chair and changed my plate, while his father sat at the head of the table. Anywhere else the son would have been waited on, but in his father's house he thought, and rightly, that it was an honour to wait.

Such are Swiss customs, of which persons of superficial understanding very foolishly make a jest. All the same, the vaunted honour and loyalty of the Swiss do not prevent them from fleecing strangers, at least as much as the Dutch, but the greenhorns who let themselves be cheated, learn thereby that it is well to bargain before-hand, and then they treat one well and charge reasonably. In this way, when I was at Bale, I baffled the celebrated Imhoff, the landlord of the "Three Kings."

M. Ote complimented me on my waiter's disguise, and said he was sorry not to have seen me officiating, nevertheless, he said he thought I was wise not to repeat the jest. He thanked me for the honour I had done his house, and begged me to do him the additional favour of dining at his table some day before I left. I answered that I would dine with him with pleasure that very day. I did so, and was treated like a prince.

The reader will have guessed that the last look my charmer gave me had not extinguished the fire which the first sight of her had kindled in my breast. It had rather increased my flame by giving me hopes of being better acquainted with her; in short, it inspired me with the idea of going to Soleure in order to give a happy ending to the adventure. I took a letter of credit on Geneva, and wrote to Madame d'Urfe, begging her to give me a written introduction, couched in strong terms to M. de Chavigni, the French ambassador, telling her that the interests of our order were highly involved in my knowing this diplomatist, and requesting her to address letters to me at the post office at Soleure. I also wrote to the Duke of Wurtemburg, but had no answer from him, and indeed he must have found my epistle very unpleasant reading.

I visited the old woman whom Giustiniani had told me of several times before I left Zurich, and although I ought to have been well satisfied as far as physical beauty was concerned, my enjoyment was very limited, as the nymphs I wooed only spoke Swiss dialect—a rugged corruption of German. I have always found that love without speech gives little enjoyment, and I cannot imagine a more unsatisfactory mistress than a mute, were she as lovely as Venus herself.

I had scarcely left Zurich when I was obliged to stop at Baden to have the carriage M. Ote had got me mended. I might have started again at eleven, but on hearing that a young Polish lady on her way to Our Lady of Einseidel was to dine at the common table, I decided to wait; but I had my trouble for nothing, as she turned out to be quite unworthy of the delay.

After dinner, while my horses were being put in, the host's daughter, a pretty girl enough, came into the room and made me waltz with her; it chanced to be a Sunday. All at once her father came in, and the girl fled.

"Sir," said the rascal, "you are condemned to pay a fine of one louis."

"Why?"

"For having danced on a holy day."

"Get out; I won't pay."

"You will pay, though," said he, shewing me a great parchment covered with writing I did not understand.

"I will appeal."

"To whom, sir?"

"To the judge of the place."

He left the room, and in a quarter of an hour I was told that the judge was waiting for me in an adjoining chamber. I thought to myself that the judges were very polite in that part of the world, but when I got into the room I saw the rascally host buried in a wig and gown.

"Sir," said he, "I am the judge."

"Judge and plaintiff too, as far as I can see."

He wrote in his book, confirming the sentence, and mulcting me in six francs for the costs of the case.

"But if your daughter had not tempted me." said I, "I should not have danced; she is therefore as guilty as I."

"Very true, sir; here is a Louis for her." So saying he took a Louis out of his pocket, put it into a desk beside him, and said; "Now yours."

I began to laugh, paid my fine, and put off my departure till the morrow.

As I was going to Lucerne I saw the apostolic nuncio (who invited me to dinner), and at Fribourg Comte d'Afri's young and charming wife; but at ten leagues from Soleure I was a witness of the following curious circumstances.

I was stopping the night in a village, and had made friends with the surgeon, whom I had found at the inn, and while supper, which he was to share with me, was getting ready, we walked about the village together. It was in the dusk of the evening, and at a distance of a hundred paces I saw a man climbing up the wall of a house, and finally vanishing through a window on the first floor.

"That's a robber," said I, pointing him out to the surgeon. He laughed and said,—

"The custom may astonish you, but it is a common one in many parts of Switzerland. The man you have just seen is a young lover who is going to pass the night with his future bride. Next morning he will leave more ardent than before, as she will not allow him to go too far. If she was weak enough to yield to his desires he would probably decline to marry her, and she would find it difficult to get married at all."

At Soleure I found a letter from Madame d'Urfe, with an enclosure from the Duc de Choiseul to the ambassador, M. de Chavigni. It was sealed, but the duke's name was written below the address.

I made a Court toilet, took a coach, and went to call on the ambassador. His excellency was not at home, so I left my card and the letter. It was a feast-day, and I went to high mass, not so much, I confess, to seek for God as for my charmer, but she was not there. After service I walked around the town, and on my return found an officer who asked me to dinner at the ambassador's.

Madame d'Urfe said that on the receipt of my letter she had gone straightway to Versailles, and that with the help of Madame de Grammont she had got me an introduction of the kind I wanted. This was good news for me, as I desired to cut an imposing figure at Soleure. I had plenty of money, and I knew that this magic metal glittered in the eyes of all. M. de Chavigni had been ambassador at Venice thirty years before, and I knew a number of anecdotes about his adventures there, and I was eager to see what I could make out of him.

I went to his house at the time appointed, and found all his servants in full livery, which I looked upon as a happy omen. My name was not announced, and I remarked that when I came in both sides of the door were opened for me by the page. A fine old man came forward to meet me, and paying me many well-turned compliments introduced me to those present. Then, with the delicate tact of the courtier, pretending not to recollect my name, he drew the Duc de Choiseul's letter from his pocket, and read aloud the paragraph in which the minister desired him to treat me with the utmost consideration. He made me sit on an easy chair at his right hand, and asked me questions to which I could only answer that I was travelling for my pleasure, and that I considered the Swiss nation to be in many respects superior to all other nations whatsoever.

Dinner was served, and his excellency set me on his right hand in a position of equal honour to his own. We were sixteen in company, and behind every chair stood a magnificent lackey in the ambassador's livery. In the course of conversation I got an opportunity of telling the ambassador that he was still spoken of at Venice with the utmost affection.

"I shall always remember," he said, "the kindness with which the Venetians treated me; but tell me, I beg, the names of those gentlemen who still remember me; they must be quite old now."

This was what I was waiting for. M. de Malipiero had told me of certain events which had happened during the regency, and M. de Bragadin had informed me of the ambassador's amours with the celebrated Stringhetta.

His excellency's fare was perfect, but in the pleasure of conversing I forgot that of eating. I told all my anecdotes so racily that his features expressed the pleasure I was affording him, and when we rose from the table he shook me by the hand, and told me he had not had so agreeable a dinner since he had been at Soleure.

"The recollection of my Venetian gallantries," said the worthy old man, "makes me recall many a happy moment; I feel quite young again."

He embraced me, and bade me consider myself as one of his family during my stay at Soleure.

After dinner he talked a good deal about Venice, praising the Government, and saying that there was not a town in the world where a man could fare better, provided he took care to get good oil and foreign wines. About five o'clock he asked me to come for a drive with him, getting into the carriage first to give me the best place.

We got out at a pretty country house where ices were served to us. On our way back he said that he had a large party every evening, and that he hoped I would do him the honour to be present whenever it suited my inclinations, assuring me that he would do his best to amuse me. I was impatient to take part in the assembly, as I felt certain I should see my charmer there. It was a vain hope, however, for I saw several ladies, some old and ugly, some passable, but not one pretty.

Cards were produced, and I soon found myself at a table with a young lady of fair complexion and a plain-looking woman well advanced in years, who seemed, however, not to be destitute of wit. Though I was looed I played on, and I lost five or six hundred fish without opening my lips. When it came to a profit and loss account, the plain woman told me I owed three louis.

"Three louis, madam."

"Yes, sir; we have been playing at two sous the fish. You thought, perhaps, we were playing for farthings."

"On the contrary, I thought it was for francs, as I never play lower." She did not answer this boast of mine, but she seemed annoyed. On rejoining the company after this wearisome game, I proceeded to scrutinize all the ladies present rapidly but keenly, but I could not see her for whom I looked, and was on the point of leaving, when I happened to notice two ladies who were looking at me attentively. I recognized them directly. They were two of my fair one's companions, whom I had had the honour of waiting on at Zurich. I hurried off, pretending not to recognize them.

Next day, a gentleman in the ambassador's suite came to tell me that his excellency was going to call on me. I told him that I would not go out till I had the honour of receiving his master, and I conceived the idea of questioning him concerning that which lay next to my heart. However, he spared me the trouble, as the reader will see for himself.

I gave M. de Chavigni the best reception I could, and after we had discussed the weather he told me, with a smile, that he had the most ridiculous affair to broach to me, begging me to credit him when he said that he did not believe it for a moment.

"Proceed, my lord."

"Two ladies who saw you at my house yesterday told me in confidence, after you had gone, that I should do well to be on my guard, as you were the waiter in an inn at Zurich where they had stayed. They added that they had seen the other waiter by the Aar, and that in all probability you had run away from the inn together; God alone knows why! They said, furthermore, that you slipped away from my house yesterday as soon as you saw them. I told them that even if you were not the bearer of a letter from his grace the Duc de Choiseul I should have been convinced that they were mistaken, and that they should dine with you to-day, if they would accept my invitation. I also hinted that you might have merely disguised yourself as a waiter in the hopes of winning some favours from them, but they rejected the hypothesis as absurd, and said that you could carve a capon and change a plate dexterously enough, but were only a common waiter for all that, adding that with my permission they would compliment you on your skill to-day.

"'Do so, by all means, ladies,' said I, 'M. Casanova and myself will be highly amused.' And now do you mind telling me whether there be any foundation of truth in the whole story?"

"Certainly, my lord, I will tell you all without reserve, but in confidence, as this ridiculous report may injure the honour of one who is dear to me, and whom I would not injure for the world."

"It is true, then? I am quite interested to hear all about it."

"It is true to a certain extent; I hope you don't take me for the real waiter at the 'Sword.'"

"Certainly not, but I supposed you played the part of waiter?"

"Exactly. Did they tell you that they were four in company."

"Ah, I have got it! Pretty Madame was one of the party. That explains the riddle; now I understand everything. But you were quite right in saying that discretion was needful; she has a perfectly blameless reputation."

"Ah! I did not know that. What happened was quite innocent, but it might be so garbled in the telling as to become prejudicial to the honour of a lady whose beauty struck me with admiration."

I told him all the details of the case, adding that I had only come to
Soleure in the hopes of succeeding in my suit.

"If that prove an impossibility," said I, "I shall leave Soleure in three or four days; but I will first turn the three ugly companions of my charmer into ridicule. They might have had sense enough to guess that the waiter's apron was only a disguise. They can only pretend to be ignorant of the fact in the hope of getting some advantage over me, and injuring their friend, who was ill advised to let them into the secret."

"Softly, softly, you go too fast and remind me of my own young days. Permit me to embrace you, your story has delighted me. You shall not go away, you shall stay here and court your charmer. To-day you can turn two mischievous women into ridicule, but do it in an easy way. The thing is so straightforward that M.—— will be the first to laugh at it. His wife cannot be ignorant of your love for her, and I know enough of women to pronounce that your disguise cannot have displeased her. She does know of your love?"

"Undoubtedly."

He went away laughing, and at the door of his coach embraced me for the third time.

I could not doubt that my charmer had told the whole story to her three friends as they were returning from Einsiedel to Zurich, and this made the part they had played all the more ill-natured; but I felt that it was to my interest to let their malice pass for wit.

I went to the ambassador's at half-past one, and after making my bow to him I proceeded to greet the company, and saw the two ladies. Thereupon, with a frank and generous air, I went up to the more malicious-looking of the two (she was lame, which may have made me think her more ill-looking) and asked if she recognized me.

"You confess, then, that you are the waiter at the 'Sword'?"

"Well, not quite that, madam, but I confess that I was the waiter for an hour, and that you cruelly disdained to address a single word to me, though I was only a waiter, because I longed for the bliss of seeing you. But I hope I shall be a little more fortunate here, and that you will allow me to pay you my respectful homage."

"This is very wonderful! You played your part so well that the sharpest eye would have been deceived. Now we shall see if you play your new part as well. If you do me the honour to call on me I will give you a good welcome."

After these complimentary speeches, the story became public property, and the whole table was amusing itself with it, when I had the happiness of seeing M.—— and Madame coming into the room.

"There is the good-natured waiter," said she to her husband.

The worthy man stepped forward, and politely thanked me for having done his wife the honour of taking off her boots.

This told me that she had concealed nothing, and I was glad. Dinner was served, M. de Chavigni made my charmer sit at his right hand, and I was placed between my two calumniators. I was obliged to hide my game, so, although I disliked them intensely, I made love to them, hardly raising my eyes to glance at Madame, who looked ravishing. I did not find her husband either as old or as jealous as I had expected. The ambassador asked him and his wife to stay the evening to an impromptu ball, and then said, that in order for me to be able to tell the Duc de Choiseul that I was well amused at Soleure, he would be delighted to have a play, if

Madame would act the fair 'Ecossaise' again. She said she should be delighted, but two more actors were wanted.

"That is all right," said the kind old gentleman, "I will play Montrose."

"And I, Murray," I remarked.

My lame friend, angry at this arrangement, which only left her the very bad part of Lady Alton, could not help lancing a shaft at me.

"Oh! why isn't there a waiter's part in the play?" said she, "you would play it so well."

"That is well said, but I hope you will teach me to play Murray even better."

Next morning, I got the words of my part, and the ambassador told me that the ball would be given in my honour. After dinner I went to my inn, and after making an elaborate toilette I returned to the brilliant company.

The ambassador begged me to open the ball, and introduced me to the highest born but not the most beautiful lady in the place. I then danced with all the ladies present until the good-natured old man got me the object of my vows as a partner in the quadrilles, which he did so easily that no one could have made any remark. "Lord Murray," said he, "must dance with no one but Lindane."

At the first pause I took the opportunity of saying that I had only come to Soleure for her sake, that it was for her sake that I had disguised myself at Zurich, and that I hoped she would permit me to pay my addresses to her.

"I cannot invite you to my house," said she, "for certain sufficient reasons; but if you will stay here some time we shall be able to see each other. But I entreat you not to shew me any marked attention in public, for there are those who will spy upon our actions, and it is not pleasant to be talked about."

I was quite satisfied with this, and told her that I would do all in my power to please her, and that the most prying eyes should have nothing to fix on. I felt that the pleasure I looked forward to would be rendered all the sweeter by a tincture of mystery.

I had proclaimed myself as a novice in the mimic art, and had entreated my lame friend to be kind enough to instruct me. I therefore went to her in the morning, but she could only flatter herself that hers was a reflected light, as I had opportunities for paying my court to my charmer in her house, and however great her vanity may have been, she must have had some suspicions of the truth.

This woman was a widow, aged between thirty and forty years, of a jaundiced complexion, and a piercing and malicious aspect. In her efforts to hide the inequality of her legs, she walked with a stiff and awkward air; and, wishing to be thought a wit, she increased her natural dullness by a ceaseless flow of small talk. I persisted in behaving towards her with a great air of respect, and one day she said that, having seen me in the disguise of a waiter, she would not have thought I was a man of a timid nature.

"In what respect do you think me timid?" said I; to which she gave me no answer, but I knew perfectly well what she meant. I was tired of my part, and I had determined to play it no more when we had acted L'Ecossaise.

All the best people at Soleure were present at our first performance. The lame lady was delighted with the horror inspired by her acting; but she might credit a great deal of it to her appearance. M. de Chavigni drew forth the tears of the audience, his acting was said to be better than the great Voltaire's. As for me, I remember how near I was to fainting when, in the third scene of the fifth act, Lindane said to me,

"What! You! You dare to love me?"

She pronounced these words with such fiery scorn that all the spectators applauded vehemently. I was almost put out of countenance, for I thought I detected in her voice an insult to my honour. However, I collected myself in the minute's respite which the loud applause gave me, and I replied,—-

"Yes; I adore you! How should I not?"

So pathetically and tenderly did I pronounce these words that the hall rang again with the applause, and the encores from four hundred throats made me repeat the words which, indeed, came from my heart.

In spite of the pleasure we had given to the audience, we judged ourselves not perfect in our parts, and M. de Chavigni advised us to put off our second performance for a couple of days.

"We will have a rehearsal to-morrow at my country house," said he, "and I beg the favour of all your companies to dinner there."

However, we all made each other compliments on our acting. My lame friend told me I had played well, but not so well as in the part of waiter, which really suited me admirably. This sarcasm got the laugh on her side, but I returned it by telling her that my performance was a work of art, while her playing of Lady Alton was pure nature. M. de Chavigni told Madame that the spectators were wrong to applaud when she expressed her wonder at my loving her, since she had spoken the words disdainfully; and it was impossible that Lindane could have despised Murray. The ambassador called for me the next day in his carriage, and when we reached his country-house we found all the actors assembled there. His excellency addressed himself in the first place to M.——, telling him he thought his business was as good as done, and that they would talk about it after dinner. We sat down to table, and afterwards rehearsed the piece without any need of the prompter's assistance.

Towards evening the ambassador told the company that he would expect them to supper that evening at Soleure, and everyone left with the exception of the ambassador, myself, and M.—— and Madame——. Just as we were going I had an agreeable surprise.

"Will you come with me," said the Ambassador to M.——, "we can talk the matter over at our ease? M. Casanova will have the honour of keeping your wife company in your carriage."

I gave the fair lady my hand respectfully, and she took it with an air of indifference, but as I was helping her in she pressed my hand with all her might. The reader can imagine how that pressure made my blood circulate like fire in my veins.

Thus we were seated side by side, our knees pressed tenderly against each other. Half an hour seemed like a minute, but it must not be thought that we wasted the time. Our lips were glued together, and were not set apart till we came within ten paces of the ambassador's house, which I could have wished at ten leagues distance. She was the first to get down, and I was alarmed to see the violent blush which overspread her whole face. Such redness looked unnatural; it might betray us; our spring of happiness would soon be dry. The watchful eye of the envious Alton would be fixed upon us, and not in vain; her triumph would outweigh her humiliation. I was at my wits' end.

Love and luck, which have so favoured me throughout the course of my life, came to my aid. I had about me a small box containing hellebore. I opened it as if by instinct, and invited her to take a small pinch. She did so, and I followed her example; but the dose was too strong, and as we were going up the stairs we began to sneeze, and for the next quarter of an hour we continued sneezing. People were obliged to attribute her high colour to the sneezing, or at least no one could give voice to any other suppositions. When the sneezing fit was over, this woman, who was as clever as she was pretty, said her headache was gone, but she would take care another time not to take so strong a dose. I looked out of the corner of my eye at the malicious widow, who said nothing but seemed deep in thought.

This piece of good luck decided me on staying at Soleure till my love was crowned with success, and I determined to take a country house. I shall not have much opinion of my readers if they find themselves in my position—rich, young, independent, full of fire, and having only pleasure to seek for—and do not follow my example. A perfect beauty was before me with whom I was madly in love, and who, I was sure, shared that love. I had plenty of money, and I was my own master. I thought this a much better plan than turning monk, and I was above caring "what people would say." As soon as the ambassador had returned, which he always did at an early hour on account of his advanced age, I left the company and went to see him in his private room. In truth I felt I must give him that confidence which he had so well deserved.

As soon as he saw me he said,—

"Well, well, did you profit by the interview I got you?"

I embraced him, and said,—

"I may hope for everything."

When I was telling him about the hellebore he was lavish in his compliments on my presence of mind, for, as he said, such an unusual colour would have made people think there had been some kind of a combat—a supposition which would not have tended towards my success. After I had told him all, I imparted my plan.

"I shall do nothing in a hurry," said I, "as I have to take care that the lady's honour does not suffer, and I trust to time to see the accomplishment of my wishes. I shall want a pretty country house, a good carriage, two lackeys, a good cook, and a housekeeper. All that I leave to your excellency, as I look upon you as my refuge and guardian angel."

"To-morrow, without fail, I will see what I can do, and I have good hopes of doing you a considerable service and of rendering you well content with the attractions of Soleure."

Next day our rehearsal went off admirably, and the day after the ambassador spoke to me as follows:

"So far as I can see, what you are aiming at in this intrigue is the satisfying of your desires without doing any harm to the lady's reputation. I think I know the nature of your love for her well enough to say that if she told you that your leaving Soleure was necessary to her peace of mind you would leave her at once. You see that I have sounded you well enough to be a competent adviser in this delicate and important affair, to which the most famous events in the annals of diplomacy are not to be compared."

"Your excellency does not do sufficient justice to a career which has gained you such distinction."

"That's because I am an old man, my dear fellow, and have shaken off the rust and dust of prejudices, and am able to see things as they really are, and appreciate them at their true value. But let us return to your love-affair. If you wish to keep it in the dark, you must avoid with the greatest care any action which may awaken suspicion in the minds of people who do not believe that anything is indifferent. The most malicious and censorious will not be able to get anything but the merest chance out of the interview I procured you today, and the accident of the sneezing bout, defy the most ill-natured to draw any deductions; for an eager lover does not begin his suit by sending the beloved one into convulsions. Nobody can guess that your hellebore was used to conceal the blush that your caresses occasioned, since it does not often happen that an amorous combat leaves such traces; and how can you be expected to have foreseen the lady's blushes, and to have provided yourself with a specific against them? In short, the events of to-day will not disclose your secret. M.—— who, although he wishes to pass for a man devoid of jealousy, is a little jealous; M.—— himself cannot have seen anything out of the common in my asking him to return with me, as I had business of importance with him, and he has certainly no reasons for supposing that I should be likely to help you to intrigue with his wife. Furthermore, the laws of politeness would have forbidden me, under any circumstances, offering the lady the place I offered him, and as he prides himself on his politeness he can raise no possible objection to the arrangement which was made. To be sure I am old and you are young—a distinction not unimportant in a husband's eyes." After this exordium, added the good-natured ambassador, with a laugh, "an exordium which I have delivered in the official style of a secretary of state, let us see where we are. Two things are necessary for you to obtain your wished-for bliss. The first thing, which concerns you more particularly, is to make M.—— your friend, and to conceal from him that you have conceived a passion for his wife, and here I will aid you to the best of my ability. The second point concerns the lady's honour; all your relations with her must appear open and above-board. Consider yourself under my protection; you must not even take a country house before we have found out some plan for throwing dust into the eyes of the observant. However, you need not be anxious; I have hit upon a plan.

"You must pretend to be taken ill, but your illness must be of such a kind that your doctor will be obliged to take your word for the symptoms. Luckily, I know a doctor whose sole idea is to order country air for all complaints. This physician, who is about as clever as his brethren, and kills or cures as well as any of them, will come and feel my pulse one of these days. You must take his advice, and for a couple of louis he will write you a prescription with country air as the chief item. He will then inform everybody that your case is serious, but that he will answer for your cure."

"What is his name?"

"Doctor Herrenschwand."

"What is he doing here? I knew him at Paris; he was Madame du Rumain's doctor."

"That is his brother. Now find out some polite complaint, which will do you credit with the public. It will be easy enough to find a house, and I will get you an excellent cook to make your gruel and beef-tea."

The choice of a complaint cost me some thought; I had to give it a good deal of attention. The same evening I managed to communicate my plan to Madame who approved of it. I begged her to think of some way of writing to me, and she said she would.

"My husband," said she, "has a very high opinion of you. He has taken no offence at our coming in the same carriage. But tell me, was it an accident or design that made M. de Chavigni take my husband and leave us together?"

"It was the result of design, dearest." She raised her beautiful eyes and bit her lips. "Are you sorry it was so?"

"Alas! no."

In three or four days, on the day on which we were going to act L'Ecossaise, the doctor came to dine with the ambassador and stayed till the evening to see the play. At dessert he complimented me on my good health, on which I took the opportunity, and told him that appearances were deceitful, and that I should be glad to consult him the next day. No doubt he was delighted to be deceived in his estimate of my health, and he said he should be glad if he could be of any service. He called on me at the hour agreed upon, and I told him such symptoms as my fancy dictated; amongst other things, that I was subject to certain nocturnal irritations which made me extremely weak, especially in the reins.

"Quite so, quite so; it's a troublesome thing, but we will see what can be done. My first remedy, which you may possibly not care much for, is for you to pass six weeks in the country, where you will not see those objects which impress your brain, acting on the seventh pair of nerves, and causing that lumbar discharge which no doubt leaves you in a very depressed state."

"Yes, it certainly does."

"Quite so, quite so. My next remedy is cold bathing."

"Are the baths far from here?"

"They are wherever you like. I will write you a prescription, and the druggist will make it up."

I thanked him, and after he had pouched the double-louis I slipped politely into his hand, he went away assuring me that I should soon experience an improvement in my health. By the evening the whole town knew that I was ill and had to go into the country. M. de Chavigni said pleasantly at dinner to the doctor, that he should have forbidden me all feminine visitors; and my lame friend, refining on the idea, added that I should above all be debarred access to certain portraits, of which I had a box-full. I laughed approvingly, and begged M. de Chavigni, in the presence of the company, to help me to find a pretty house and a good cook, as I did not intend to take my meals alone.

I was tired of playing a wearisome part, and had left off going to see my lame friend, but she soon reproached me for my inconstancy, telling me that I had made a tool of her. "I know all," said this malicious woman, "and I will be avenged."

"You cannot be avenged for nothing," said I, "for I have never done you an injury. However, if you intend to have me assassinated, I shall apply for police protection."

"We don't assassinate here," said she, savagely. "We are not Italians."

I was delighted to be relieved from the burden of her society, and henceforth Madame was the sole object of my thoughts. M. de Chavigni, who seemed to delight in serving me, made her husband believe that I was the only person who could get the Duc de Choiseul to pardon a cousin of his who was in the guards, and had had the misfortune to kill his man in a duel. "This," said the kindly old gentleman, "is the best way possible of gaining the friendship of your rival. Do you think you can manage it?"

"I am not positive of success."

"Perhaps I have gone a little too far; but I told him that by means of your acquaintance with the Duchesse de Grammont you could do anything with the minister."

"I must make you a true prophet; I will do all I can."

The consequence was that M.—— informed me of the facts in the ambassador's presence, and brought me all the papers relative to the case.

I spent the night in writing to the Duchesse de Grammont. I made my letter as pathetic as possible, with a view to touching her heart, and then her father's; and I then wrote to the worthy Madame d'Urfe telling her that the well-being of the sublime order of the Rosy Cross was concerned in the pardon of a Swiss officer, who had been obliged to leave the kingdom on account of a duel in which the order was highly concerned.

In the morning, after resting for an hour, I went to the ambassador, and shewed him the letter I had written to the duchess. He thought it excellently expressed, and advised me to skew it to M.—— I found him with his night-cap on; he was extremely grateful for the interest I took in a matter which was so near to his heart. He told me that his wife had not yet risen, and asked me to wait and take breakfast with her. I should have much liked to accept the invitation, but I begged him to make my excuses to his lady for my absence, on the pretence that I had to finish my letters, and hand them to the courier who was just leaving. I hoped in this way to scatter any jealousy that might be hovering in his brain, by the slight importance I attached to a meeting with his wife.

I went to dine with M. de Chavigni, who thought my conduct had been very politic, and said that he was certain that henceforth M.—— would be my best friend. He then skewed me a letter from Voltaire thanking him for playing Montrose in his Ecossaise; and another from the Marquis de Chauvelin, who was then at Delices with the philosopher of Ferney. He promised to come and see him after he had been to Turin, where he had been appointed ambassador.

CHAPTER XV

My Country House—Madame Dubois—Malicious Trick Played on Me by My Lame Enemy—My Vexation

There was a reception and a supper at the Court, as they styled the hotel of M. de Chavigni, or rather of the ambassador of the King of France in Switzerland. As I came in I saw my charmer sitting apart reading a letter. I accosted her, apologizing for not having stayed to breakfast, but she said I had done quite right, adding that if I had not chosen a country house she hoped I would take one her husband would probably mention to me that evening. She could not say any more, as she was called away to a game at quadrille. For my part I did not play, but wandered from one table to another.

At supper everybody talked to me about my health, and my approaching stay in the country. This gave M.—— an opportunity to mention a delightful house near the Aar; "but," he added, "it is not to be let for less than six months."

"If I like it," I replied, "and am free to leave it when I please, I will willingly pay the six months' rent in advance."

"There is a fine hall in it."

"All the better; I will give a ball as evidence of my gratitude to the people of Soleure for the kind welcome I have received from them."

"Would you like to come and see it to-morrow?"

"With pleasure."

"Very good, then I will call for you at eight o'clock, if that hour will suit you."

"I shall expect you."

When I got back to my lodging I ordered a travelling carriage and four, and the next morning, before eight o'clock, I called for M. who was ready, and seemed flattered at my anticipating him.

"I made my wife promise to come with us; but she is a sluggard, who prefers her bed to the fresh air."

In less than an hour we reached our journey's end, and I found the house a beautiful one and large enough to lodge the whole court of a prince of the Holy Roman Empire. Besides the hall, which I thought magnificent, I noted with great pleasure a closet arranged as a boudoir, and covered with the most exquisite pictures. A fine garden, fountains, baths, several well-furnished rooms, a good kitchen—in a word, everything pleased me, and I begged M.—— to arrange for me to take up my abode there in two days' time.

When we got back to Soleure, Madame told me how pleased she was that I liked the house; and seizing the opportunity, I said that I hoped they would often do me the honour of dining with me. They promised they would do so. I drew from my pocket a packet containing a hundred louis, which I gave M.—— to pay the rent. I then embraced him, and after imprinting a respectful kiss on the hand of his fair mate I went to M. de Chavigni, who approved of my having taken the house as it pleased my lady, and asked me if it was true that I was going to give a ball.

"Yes, if I see any prospect of its being a brilliant one, and if I have your approbation."

"You need have no doubts on that point, my dear fellow, and whatever you can't find in the shops come to me for. Come, I see you are going to spend a little money. It is a good plan, and overcomes many difficulties. In the meanwhile you shall have two footmen, an excellent cook, a housekeeper, and whatever other servants you require. The head of my household will pay them, and you can settle with him afterwards, he is a trustworthy man. I will come now and then and take a spoonful of soup with you, and you shall reward me for what services I may have done you by telling me how things are getting on. I have a great esteem for your charming friend, her discretion is beyond her years, and the pledges of love you will obtain of her will doubtless increase your passion and your esteem. Is she aware that I know all?"

"She knows that we are firm friends, and she is glad of it, as she is sure that you will be discreet."

"She may count on my discretion. She is really a delicious woman; I should have been tempted to seduce her myself thirty years ago."

A druggist, whom the doctor had recommended to me, set out the same day to get ready the baths which were to cure me of my imaginary complaint, and in two days I went myself, after having given Le Duc orders to bring my baggage on.

I was extremely surprised, on entering the apartment I was to occupy, to see a pretty young woman who came up to me in a modest way to kiss my hand. I stopped her doing so, and my astonished air made her blush.

"Do you belong to the household?" I said.

"The ambassador's steward has engaged me as your housekeeper."

"Pardon my surprise. Take me to my room."

She obeyed, and sitting down on the couch I begged her to sit beside me.

"That is an honour," said she, in the most polite and modest way, "I cannot allow myself. I am only your servant."

"Very good, but when I am alone I hope you will consent to take your meals with me, as I don't like eating by myself."

"I will do so, sir."

"Where is your room?"

"This is the one the steward assigned to me, but you have only to speak if you wish me to sleep in another."

"Not at all; it will do very well."

Her room was just behind the recess in which my bed stood. I went in with her and was astonished to see a great display of dresses, and in an adjoining closet all the array of the toilette, linen in abundance, and a good stock of shoes and embroidered slippers. Dumb with surprise I looked at her, and was thoroughly satisfied with what I saw. Nevertheless I determined to subject her to a close examination, as I thought her manners too interesting and her linen too extensive for her to be a mere servant. All at once I was struck with the idea that it might be a trick of the ambassador's, for a fine woman, well educated, and aged twenty-four or at the most twenty-five years, seemed to me more fitted to be my mistress than my housekeeper. I therefore asked her if she knew the ambassador, and what wages she was to receive. She replied that she only knew M. de Chavigni by sight, and that the steward had promised her two louis a month and her meals in her own room.

"Where do you come from? What's your name?"

"I come from Lyons; I am a widow, and my name is Dubois."

"I am delighted to have you in my service. I shall see you again."

She then left me, and I could not help thinking her a very interesting woman, as her speech was as dignified as her appearance. I went down to the kitchen and found the cook, an honest-looking fellow, who told me his name was Rosier. I had known his brother in the service of the French ambassador at Venice. He told me that supper would be ready at nine o'clock.

"I never eat by myself," said I.

"So I hear, sir; and I will serve supper accordingly."

"What are your wages?"

"Four louis a month."

I then went to see the rest of my people. I found two sharp-looking footmen, and the first of them told me he would see I had what wine I wanted. Then I inspected my bath, which seemed convenient. An apothecary was preparing certain matters for my imaginary cure. Finally, I took a walk round my garden, and before going in I went into the gate-keeper's, where I found a numerous family, and some girls who were not to be despised. I was delighted to hear everybody speak French, and I talked with them some time.

When I got back to my room, I found Le Duc occupied in unpacking my mails; and telling him to give my linen to Madame Dubois, I went into a pretty cabinet adjoining, where there was a desk and all materials necessary for writing. This closet had only one window facing north, but it commanded a view capable of inspiring the finest thoughts. I was amusing myself with the contemplation of this sublime prospect, when I heard a knock at my door. It was my pretty housekeeper, who wore a modest and pleasant expression, and did not in the least resemble a person who bears a complaint.

"What can I do for you, madam?"

"I hope you will be good enough to order your man to be polite to me?"

"Certainly; how has he failed in politeness?"

"He might possibly tell you in no respect. He wanted to kiss me, and as I refused he thought himself justified in being rather insolent."

"How?"

"By laughing at me. You will pardon me, sir, but I do not like people who make game."

"You are right; they are sure to be either silly or malicious. Make yourself easy; Le Duc shall understand that you are to be treated with respect. You will please sup with me."

Le Duc came in soon after, and I told him to behave respectfully towards
Madame Dubois.

"She's a sly cat," said the rascal; "she wouldn't let me kiss her."

"I am afraid you are a bad fellow."

"Is she your servant or your mistress?"

"She might be my wife."

"Oh! well, that's different. That will do; Madame Dubois shall have all respect, and I will try my luck somewhere else."

I had a delicious supper. I was contented with my cook, my butler, my housekeeper, and even with my Spaniard, who waited capitally at table.

After supper I sent out Le Duc and the other servant, and as soon as I was alone with my too lovely housekeeper, who had behaved at table like a woman of the world, I begged her to tell me her history.

"My history, sir, is short enough, and not very interesting. I was—born at Lyons, and my relations took me to Lausanne, as I have been told, for I was too young at the time to remember anything about it. My father, who was in the service of Madame d'Ermance, left me an orphan when I was fourteen. Madame d'Ermance was fond of me, and knowing that my mother's means were small she took me to live with her. I had attained my seventeenth year when I entered the service of Lady Montagu as lady's maid, and some time after I was married to Dubois, an old servant of the house. We went to England, and three years after my marriage I lost my husband. The climate of England affected my lungs, and I was obliged to beg my lady to allow me to leave her service. The worthy lady saw how weak I was, and paid the expenses of my journey and loaded me with rich presents. I returned to my mother at Lausanne, where my health soon returned, and I went into the service of an English lady who was very fond of me, and would have taken me with her to Italy if she had not conceived some suspicions about the young Duke of Rosebury, with whom she was in love, and whom she thought in love with me. She suspected me, but wrongfully, of being her rival in secret. She sent me away, after giving me rich presents, and saying how sorry she was she could not keep me. I went back to my mother, and for two years I have lived with the toil of my hands. Four days ago M. Lebel, the ambassador's steward, asked me if I would enter the service of an Italian gentleman as housekeeper. I agreed, in the hope of seeing Italy, and this hope is the cause of my stupidity. In short: here I am."

"What stupidity are you referring to?"

"The stupidity of having entered your service before I knew you."

"I like your freedom. You would not have come, then, if you had not known me?"

"Certainly not, for no lady will ever take me after having been with you."

"Why not? may I ask."

"Well, sir; do you think you are the kind of man to have a house-keeper like myself without the public believing my situation to be of quite a different nature?"

"No, you are too pretty, and I don't look like a fossil, certainly; but after all, what matter does it make?"

"It is all very well for you to make light of it, and if I were in your place I would do the same; but how am I, who am a woman and not in an independent position, to set myself above the rules and regulations of society?"

"You mean, Madame Dubois, that you would very much like to go back to Lausanne?"

"Not exactly, as that would not be just to you."

"How so?"

"People would be sure to say that either your words or your deeds were too free, and you might possibly pass a rather uncharitable judgment on me."

"What judgment could I pass on you?"

"You might think I wanted to impose on you."

"That might be, as I should be very much hurt by so sudden and uncalled-for a departure. All the same I am sorry for you, as with your ideas you can neither go nor stay with any satisfaction. Nevertheless, you must do one or the other."

"I have made up my mind. I shall stay, and I am almost certain I shall not regret it."

"I am glad to hear that, but there is one point to which I wish to call your attention."

"What is that?"

"I will tell you. Let us have no melancholy and no scruples."

"You shall not see me melancholy, I promise you; but kindly explain what you mean by the word 'scruples.'"

"Certainly. In its ordinary acceptation, the word 'scruple' signifies a malicious and superstitious whim, which pronounces an action which may be innocent to be guilty."

"When a course of action seems doubtful to me, I never look upon the worst side of it. Besides, it is my duty to look after myself and not other people."

"I see you have read a good deal."

"Reading is my greatest luxury. Without books I should find life unbearable."

"Have you any books?"

"A good many. Do you understand English?"

"Not a word."

"I am sorry for that, as the English books would amuse you."

"I do not care for romances."

"Nor do I. But you don't think that there are only romances in English, do you? I like that. Why do you take me for such a lover of the romantic, pray?"

"I like that, too. That pretty outburst is quite to my taste, and I am delighted to be the first to make you laugh."

"Pardon me if I laugh, but . . ."

"But me no buts, my dear; laugh away just as you like, you will find that the best way to get over me. I really think, though, that you put your services at too cheap a rate."

"That makes me laugh again, as it is for you to increase my wages if you like."

"I shall take care that it is done."

I rose from table, not taken, but surprised, with this young woman, who seemed to be getting on my blind side. She reasoned well, and in this first interview she had made a deep impression on me. She was young, pretty, elegant, intellectual, and of distinguished manners; I could not guess what would be the end of our connection. I longed to speak to M. Lebel, to thank him for getting me such a marvel, and still more, to ask him some questions about her.

After the supper had been taken away, she came to ask if I would have my hair put in curl papers.

"It's Le Duc's business," I answered, "but if you like, it shall be yours for the future."

She acquitted herself like an expert.

"I see," said I, "that you are going to serve me as you served Lady Montagu."

"Not altogether; but as you do not like melancholy, allow me to ask a favour."

"Do so, my dear."

"Please do not ask me to give you your bath."

"Upon my honour, I did not think of doing so. It would be scandalous.
That's Le Duc's business."

"Pardon me, and allow me to ask another favour."

"Tell me everything you want."

"Allow me to have one of the door-keeper's daughters to sleep with me."

"If it had come into my head, I would have proposed it to you. Is she in your room now?"

"No."

"Go and call her, then."

"Let us leave that till to-morrow, as if I went at this time of night it might make people talk."

"I see you have a store of discretion, and you may be sure I will not deprive you of any of it."

She helped me to undress, and must have found me very modest, but I must say it was not from virtue. My heart was engaged elsewhere, and Madame Dubois had impressed me; I was possibly duped by her, but I did not trouble myself to think whether I was or not. I rang for Le Duc in the morning, and on coming in he said he had not expected the honour.

"You're a rascal," I said, "get two cups of chocolate ready directly after I have had my bath."

After I had taken my first cold bath, which I greatly enjoyed, I went to bed again. Madame Dubois came in smiling, dressed in a style of careless elegance.

"You look in good spirits."

"I am, because I am happy with you. I have had a good night, and there is now in my room a girl as lovely as an angel, who is to sleep with me."

"Call her in."

She called her, and a monster of ugliness entered, who made me turn my head away.

"You haven't given yourself a rival certainly, my dear, but if she suits you it is all right. You shall have your breakfast with me, and I hope you will take chocolate with me every morning."

"I shall be delighted, as I am very fond of it."

I had a pleasant afternoon. M. de Chavigni spent several hours with me. He was pleased with everything, and above all with my fair housekeeper, of whom Lebel had said nothing to him.

"She will be an excellent cure for your love for Madame," said he.

"There you are wrong," I answered, "she might make me fall in love with her without any diminution of my affection for my charmer."

Next day, just as I was sitting down to table with my housekeeper, I saw a carriage coming into the courtyard, and my detestable lame widow getting out of it. I was terribly put out, but the rules of politeness compelled me to go and receive her.

"I was far from anticipating that you would do me so great an honour, madam."

"I daresay; I have come to dine with you, and to ask you to do me a favour."

"Come in, then, dinner is just being served. I beg to introduce Madame
Dubois to you."

I turned towards my charming housekeeper, and told her that the lady would dine with us.

Madame Dubois, in the character of mistress of the house, did the honours admirably, and my lame friend, in spite of her pride, was very polite to her. I did not speak a dozen words during the meal, and paid no sort of attention to the detestable creature; but I was anxious to know what she could want me to do for her. As soon as Madame Dubois had left the room she told me straight out that she had come to ask me to let her have a couple of rooms in my house for three weeks or a month at the most.

I was astonished at such a piece of impudence, and told her she asked more than I was at liberty to give.

"You can't refuse me, as everybody knows I have come on purpose to ask you."

"Then everybody must know that I have refused you. I want to be alone—absolutely alone, without any kind of restriction on my liberty. The least suspicion of company would bore me."

"I shall not bore you in any way, and you will be at perfect liberty to ignore my presence. I shall not be offended if you don't enquire after me, and I shall not ask after you—even if you are ill. I shall have my meals served to me by my own servant, and I shall take care not to walk in the garden unless I am perfectly certain you are not there. You must allow that if you have any claims to politeness you cannot refuse me."

"If you were acquainted with the most ordinary rules of politeness, madam, you would not persist in a request to which I have formally declined to accede."

She did not answer, but my words had evidently produced no effect. I was choking with rage. I strode up and down the room, and felt inclined to send her away by force as a madwoman. However, I reflected that she had relations in a good position whom I might offend if I treated her roughly, and that I might make an enemy capable of exacting a terrible revenge; and, finally, that Madame might disapprove of my using violence to this hideous harpy....

"Well, madam," said I, "you shall have the apartment you have solicited with so much importunity, and an hour after you come in I shall be on my way back to Soleure."

"I accept the apartment, and I shall occupy it the day after to-morrow. As for your threat of returning to Soleure, it is an idle one, as you would thereby make yourself the laughing-stock of the whole town."

With this final impertinence she rose and went away, without taking any further notice of me. I let her go without moving from my seat. I was stupefied. I repented of having given in; such impudence was unparalleled. I called myself a fool, and vowed I deserved to be publicly hooted. I ought to have taken the whole thing as a jest; to have contrived to get her out of the house on some pretext, and then to have sent her about her business as a madwoman, calling all my servants as witnesses.

My dear Dubois came in, and I told my tale. She was thunderstruck.

"I can hardly credit her requesting, or your granting, such a thing," said she, "unless you have some motives of your own."

I saw the force of her argument, and not wishing to make a confidante of her I held my tongue, and went out to work off my bile.

I came in tired, after taking a stiff walk. I took supper with Madame Dubois, and we sat at table till midnight. Her conversation pleased me more and more; her mind was well-furnished, her speech elegant, and she told her stories and cracked her jokes with charming grace. She was devoid of prejudices, but by no means devoid of principle. Her discretion was rather the result of system than of virtue; but if she had not a virtuous spirit, her system would not have shielded her from the storms of passion or the seductions of vice.

My encounter with the impudent widow had so affected me that I could not resist going at an early hour on the following day to communicate it to M. de Chavigni. I warned Madame Dubois that if I were not back by dinner-time she was not to wait for me.

M. de Chavigni had been told by my enemy that she was going to pay me a visit, but he roared with laughter on hearing the steps she had taken to gain her ends.

"Your excellency may find it very funny," said I, "but I don't."

"So I see; but take my advice, and be the first to laugh at the adventure. Behave as if you were unaware of her presence, and that will be a sufficient punishment for her. People will soon say she is smitten with you, and that you disdain her love. Go and tell the story to M.——, and stay without ceremony to dinner. I have spoken to Lebel about your pretty housekeeper: the worthy man had no malicious intent in sending her to you. He happened to be going to Lausanne, and just before, I had told him to find you a good housekeeper; thinking it over on his way, he remembered his friend Madame Dubois, and the matter was thus arranged without malice or pretense. She is a regular find, a perfect jewel for you, and if you get taken with her I don't think she will allow you to languish for long."

"I don't know, she seems to be a woman of principle."

"I shouldn't have thought you would be taken in by that sort of thing. I will ask you both to give me a dinner to-morrow, and shall be glad to hear her chatter."

M—— welcomed me most kindly, and congratulated me on my conquest, which would make my country house a paradise. I joined in the jest, of course, with the more ease that his charming wife, though I could see that she suspected the truth, added her congratulations to those of her husband; but I soon changed the course of their friendly mirth by telling them the circumstances of the case. They were indignant enough then, and the husband said that if she had really quartered herself on me in that fashion, all I had to do was to get an injunction from the courts forbidding her to put her foot within my doors.

"I don't want to do that," said I, "as besides publicly disgracing her I should be skewing my own weakness, and proclaiming that I was not the master in my own house, and that I could not prevent her establishing herself with me."

"I think so, too," said the wife, "and I am glad you gave way to her. That shews how polite you are, and I shall go and call on her to congratulate her on the welcome she got, as she told me that her plans had succeeded."

Here the matter ended, and I accepted their invitation to dine with them. I behaved as a friend, but with that subtle politeness which takes away all ground for suspicion; accordingly, the husband felt no alarm. My charmer found the opportunity to tell me that I had done wisely in yielding to the ill-timed demand of that harpy, and that as soon as M. de Chauvelin, whom they were expecting, had gone away again, I could ask her husband to spend a few days with me, and that she would doubtless come too.

"Your door-keeper's wife," she added, "was my nurse. I have been kind to her, and when necessary I can write to you by her without running any risk."

After calling on two Italian Jesuits who were passing through Soleure, and inviting them to dine with me on the following day,

I returned home where the good Dubois amused me till midnight by philosophical discussions. She admired Locke; and maintained that the faculty of thought was not a proof of the existence of spirit in us, as it was in the power of God to endow matter with the capacity for thought; I was unable to controvert this position. She made me laugh by saying that there was a great difference between thinking and reasoning, and I had the courage to say,—

"I think you would reason well if you let yourself be persuaded to sleep with me, and you think you reason well in refusing to be so persuaded."

"Trust me, sir," said she; "there is as much difference between the reasoning powers of men and women as there is between their physical characteristics."

Next morning at nine o'clock we were taking our chocolate, when my enemy arrived. I heard her carriage, but I did not take the slightest notice. The villainous woman sent away the carriage and installed herself in her room with her maid.

I had sent Le Duc to Soleure for my letters, so I was obliged to beg my housekeeper to do my hair; and she did it admirably, as I told her we should have the ambassador and the two Jesuits to dinner. I thanked her, and kissed her for the first time on the cheek, as she would not allow me to touch her beautiful lips. I felt that we were fast falling in love with one another, but we continued to keep ourselves under control, a task which was much easier for her than for me, as she was helped by that spirit of coquetry natural to the fair sex, which often has greater power over them than love itself.

M. de Chavigni came at two; I had consulted him before asking the Jesuits, and had sent my carriage for them. While we were waiting for these gentlemen we took a turn in the garden, and M. de Chavigni begged my fair housekeeper to join us as soon as she had discharged certain petty duties in which she was then engaged.

M. de Chavigni was one of those men who were sent by France to such powers as she wished to cajole and to win over to her interests. M. de l'Hopital, who knew how to gain the heart of Elizabeth Petrovna, was another; the Duc de Nivernois, who did what he liked with the Court of St. James's in 1762, is a third instance.

Madame Dubois came out to us in due course, and entertained us very agreeably; and M. de Chavigni told me that he considered she had all the qualities which would make a man happy. At dinner she enchanted him and captivated the two Jesuits by her delicate and subtle wit. In the evening this delightful old nobleman told me he had spent a most pleasant day, and after asking me to dine at his house while M. de Chauvelin was there, he left me with an effusive embrace.

M. de Chauvelin, whom I had the honour to know at Versailles, at M. de Choiseul's, was an extremely pleasant man. He arrived at Soleure in the course of two days, and M. de Chavigni having advised me of his presence I hastened to pay my court to him. He remembered me, and introduced me to his wife, whom I had not the honour of knowing. As chance placed me next to my charmer at table, my spirits rose, and my numerous jests and stories put everybody in a good temper. On M. de Chauvelin remarking that he knew some pleasant histories of which I was the hero, M. de Chavigni told him that he did not know the best of all, and recounted to him my adventure at Zurich. M. de Chauvelin then told Madame that to serve her he would willingly transform himself into a footman, on which M.—— joined in and said that I had a finer taste for beauty, as she, for whose sake I had made myself into a waiter, was at that moment a guest of mine in my country house.

"Ah, indeed!" said M. de Chauvelin, "then we must come and see your quarters, M. Casanova."

I was going to reply, when M. de Chavigni anticipated me by saying,

"Yes, indeed! and I hope he will lend me his beautiful hall to give you a ball next Sunday."

In this manner the good-natured courtier prevented me from promising to give a ball myself, and relieved me of my foolish boast, which I should have been wrong in carrying out, as it would have been an encroachment on his privilege as ambassador of entertaining these distinguished strangers during the five or six days they might stay at Soleure. Besides, if I had kept to my word, it would have involved me in a considerable expense, which would not have helped me in my suit.

The conversation turning on Voltaire, the Ecossaise was mentioned, and the acting of my neighbour was highly commended in words that made her blush and shine in her beauty like a star, whereat her praises were renewed.

After dinner the ambassador invited us to his ball on the day after the morrow, and I went home more deeply in love than ever with my dear charmer, whom Heaven had designed to inflict on me the greatest grief I have had in my life, as the reader shall see.

I found that my housekeeper had gone to bed, and I was glad of it, for the presence of my fair one had excited my passions to such an extent that my reason might have failed to keep me within the bounds of respect. Next morning she found me sad, and rallied me in such a way that I soon recovered my spirits. While we were taking our chocolate the lame creature's maid brought me a note, and I sent her away, telling her that I would send the answer by my own servant. This curious letter ran as follows:

"The ambassador has asked me to his ball on Sunday. I answered that I was not well, but if I found myself better in the evening I would come. I think that as I am staying in your house I ought to be introduced by you or stay away altogether. So if you do not wish to oblige me by taking me, I must beg of you to tell the ambassador that I am ill. Pardon me if I have taken the liberty of infringing our agreement in this peculiar instance, but it is a question of keeping up some sort of appearance in public."

"Not so," I cried, mad with rage; and taking my pen I wrote thus:

"I think your idea is a beautiful one, madam. You will have to be ill, as I mean to keep to the conditions you made yourself, and to enjoy full liberty in all things, and I shall therefore deny myself the honour of taking you to the ball which the ambassador is to give in my hall."

I read her insolent letter and my reply to my housekeeper, who thought the answer just what she deserved. I then sent it to her.

I passed the next two days quietly and agreeably without going out or seeing any visitors, but the society of Madame Dubois was all-sufficient for me. Early on Sunday morning the ambassador's people came to make the necessary preparations for the ball and supper. Lebel came to pay me his respects while I was at table. I made him sit down, while I thanked him for procuring me a housekeeper who was all perfection.

Lebel was a fine man, middle-aged, witty, and an excellent steward, though perfectly honest.

"Which of you two," said he to me, "is the most taken in?"

"We are equally pleased with each other," answered my charming housekeeper.

To my great delight the first pair to appear were M.—— and Madame. She was extremely polite to Madame Dubois, and did not shew the slightest astonishment when I introduced her as my housekeeper. She told me that I must take her to see her lame friend, and to my great disgust I had to go. We were received with a show of great friendship, and she went out with us into the garden, taking M.——'s arm, while his wife leant amorously on mine.

When we had made a few turns of the garden, Madame begged me to take her to her nurse. As her husband was close by, I said,—

"Who is your nurse?"

"Your door-keeper's wife," said her husband, "we will wait for you in this lady's apartment."

"Tell me, sweetheart," said she on the way, "does not your pretty housekeeper sleep with you?"

"I swear she does not; I can only love you."

"I would like to believe you, but I find it hard to do so; however, if you are speaking the truth it is wrong of you to keep her in the house, as nobody will believe in your innocence."

"It is enough for me that you believe in it. I admire her, and at any other time I expect we could not sleep under the same roof without sleeping in the same bed; but now that you rule my heart I am not capable of a passion for her."

"I am delighted to hear it; but I think she is very pretty."

We went in to see her nurse, who called her "my child," and kissed her again and again, and then left us alone to prepare some lemonade for us. As soon as we found ourselves alone our mouths were glued together, and my hands touched a thousand beauties, covered only by a dress of light sarcenet; but I could not enjoy her charms without this cruel robe, which was all the worse because it did not conceal the loveliness beneath it. I am sure that the good nurse would have kept us waiting a long time if she had known how we longed to be left alone for a few moments longer; but, alas! the celerity with which she made those two glasses of lemonade was unexampled.

"It was made beforehand, was it?" said I, when I saw her coming in.

"Not at all, sir; but I am a quick hand."

"You are, indeed."

These words made my charmer go off into a peal of laughter, which she accompanied with a significant glance in my direction. As we were going away she said that as things seemed to be against us we must wait till her husband came to spend a few days with me.

My terrible enemy gave us some sweets, which she praised very highly, and above all some quince marmalade, which she insisted on our testing. We begged to be excused, and Madame pressed my foot with hers. When we had got away she told me I had been very wise not to touch anything, as the widow was suspected of having poisoned her husband.

The ball, the supper, the refreshments, and the guests were all of the most exquisite and agreeable kind. I only danced one minuet with Madame de Chauvelin, nearly all my evening being taken up with talking to her husband. I made him a present of my translation of his poem on the seven deadly sins, which he received with much pleasure.

"I intend," said I, "to pay you a visit at Turin."

"Are you going to bring your housekeeper with you?"

"No."

"You are wrong, for she is a delightful person."

Everybody spoke of my dear Dubois in the same way. She had a perfect knowledge of the rules of good breeding, and she knew how to make herself respected without being guilty of the slightest presumption. In vain she was urged to dance, and she afterwards told me that if she had yielded she would have become an object of hatred to all the ladies. She knew that she could dance exquisitely.

M. de Chauvelin went away in two days, and towards the end of the week I heard from Madame d'Urfe, who told me that she had spent two days at Versailles in furtherance of my desires. She sent me a copy of the letters of pardon signed by the king in favour of the relation of M.——, assuring me that the original had been sent to the colonel of his regiment, where he would be reinstated in the rank which he held before the duel.

I had my horses put into my carriage, and hastened to carry this good news to M. de Chavigni. I was wild with joy, and I did not conceal it from the ambassador, who congratulated me, since M.—— having obtained by me, without the expenditure of a penny, a favour which would have cost him dear if he had succeeded in purchasing it, would henceforth be only too happy to treat me with the utmost confidence.

To make the matter still more important, I begged my noble friend to announce the pardon to M.—— in person, and he immediately wrote a note to that gentleman requesting his presence.

As soon as he made his appearance, the ambassador handed him the copy of the pardon, telling him that he owed it all to me. The worthy man was in an ecstasy, and asked what he owed me.

"Nothing, sir, unless you will give me your friendship, which I value more than all the gold in the world; and if you would give me a proof of your friendship, come and spend a few days with me; I am positively dying of loneliness. The matter I have done for you is a mere trifle; you see how quickly it has been arranged."

"A mere trifle! I have devoted a year's labour to it; I have moved heaven and earth without succeeding, and in a fortnight you have accomplished it. Sir, you may dispose of my life."

"Embrace me, and come and see me. I am the happiest of men when I am enabled to serve persons of your merit."

"I will go and tell the good news to my wife, who will love you as well as I do."

"Yes, do so," said the ambassador, "and bring her to dinner here to-morrow."

When we were alone together, the Marquis de Chavigni, an old courtier and a wit, began to make some very philosophical reflections on the state of a court where nothing can be said to be easy or difficult per se, as the one at a moment's notice may become the other; a court where justice often pleads in vain, while interest or even importunity get a ready hearing. He had known Madame d'Urfe, had even paid his court to her at the period when she was secretly beloved by the regent. He it was who had given her the name of Egeria, because she said she had a genius who directed her and passed the nights with her when she slept by herself. The ambassador then spoke of M.——, who had undoubtedly become a very great friend of mine.

"The only way to blind a jealous husband," said he, "is to make him your friend, for friendship will rarely admit jealousy."

The next day at dinner, at the ambassador's, Madame gave me a thousand proofs of grateful friendship, which my heart interpreted as pledges of love. The husband and wife promised to pay me a three days' visit in the following week at my country house.

They kept their word without giving me any further warning, but I was not taken by surprise as I had made all preparations for their reception.

My heart leapt with joy on seeing my charmer getting down from the carriage, but my joy was not unalloyed, as the husband told me that they must absolutely return on the fourth day, and the wife insisted on the horrible widow being present at all our conversation.

I took my guests to the suite of rooms I had prepared for them, and which I judged most suitable for my designs. It was on the ground floor, opposite to my room. The bedroom had a recess with two beds, separated by a partition through which one passed by a door. I had the key to all the doors, and the maid would sleep in a closet beyond the ante-chamber.

In obedience to my divinity's commands we went and called on the widow, who gave us a cordial welcome; but under the pretext of leaving us in freedom refused to be of our company during the three days. However, she gave in when I told her that our agreement was only in force when I was alone.

My dear Dubois, with her knowledge of the rules of society, did not need a hint to have her supper in her room, and we had an exquisite meal as I had given orders that the fare should be of the best. After supper I took my guests to their apartment, and felt obliged to do the same by the widow. She wanted me to assist at her toilet, but I excused myself with a bow. She said, maliciously, that after all the pains I had taken I deserved to be successful. I gave her no answer.

Next morning, as we were walking in the garden, I warned my charmer that I had all the keys of the house, and that I could introduce myself into her room at any moment.

"I am waiting," said she, "for my husband's embraces, which he has prefaced with caresses, as is usual with him. We must therefore wait till the night after next, which will take away all risk, as I have never known him to embrace me for two nights in succession."

About noon we had a visit from M. de Chavigni, who came to ask for dinner, and made a great to-do when he heard that my housekeeper dined in her room. The ladies said he was quite right, so we all went and made her sit down at table with us. She must have been flattered, and the incident evidently increased her good humour, as she amused us by her wit and her piquant stories about Lady Montagu. When we had risen from table Madame said to me,—

"You really must be in love with that young woman; she is ravishing."

"If I could pass two hours in your company to-night, I would prove to you that I am yours alone."

"It is still out of the question, as my husband has ascertained that the moon changes to-day."

"He has to ask leave of the moon, has he, before discharging so sweet a duty?"

"Exactly. According to his system of astrology, it is the only way to keep his health and to have the son that Heaven wills to grant him, and indeed without aid from above it is hardly likely that his wishes will be accomplished."

"I hope to be the instrument of Heaven," said I, laughing.

"I only hope you may."

Thus I was obliged to wait. Next morning, as we were walking in the garden, she said to me,—

"The sacrifice to the moon has been performed, and to make sure I will cause him to renew his caresses tonight as soon as we go to bed; and after that he is certain to sleep soundly. You can come at an hour after midnight; love will await you."

Certain of my bliss, I gave myself up to the joy that such a certainty kindles in a fiery heart. It was the only night remaining, as M.—— had decided that on the next day they would return to Soleure.

After supper I took the ladies to their apartments, and on returning told my housekeeper that I had a good deal of writing to do, and that she should go to bed.

Just before one o'clock I left my room, and the night being a dark one I had to feel my way half round my house, and to my surprise found the door open; but I did not pay any attention to this circumstance. I opened the door of the second ante-chamber, and the moment I shut it again a hand seized mine, whilst another closed my lips. I only heard a whispered "hush!" which bade me silent. A sofa was at hand; we made it our altar of sacrifice, and in a moment I was within the temple of love. It was summer time and I had only two hours before me, so I did not lose a moment, and thinking I held between my arms the woman I had so long sighed for I renewed again and again the pledges of my ardent love. In the fulness of my bliss I thought her not awaiting me in her bed an admirable idea, as the noise of our

81

kisses and the liveliness of our motions might have awakened the troublesome husband. Her tender ecstasies equalled mine, and increased my bliss by making me believe (oh, fatal error!) that of all my conquests this was the one of which I had most reason to boast.

To my great grief the clock warned me that it was time for me to be gone. I covered her with the tenderest kisses, and returning to my room, in the greatest gladness, I resigned myself to sleep.

I was roused at nine o'clock by M.——, who seemed in a happy frame of mind, and shewed me a letter he had just received, in which his relative thanked me for restoring him to his regiment. In this letter, which was dictated by gratitude, he spoke of me as if I had been a divinity.

"I am delighted," I said, "to have been of service to you."

"And I," said he, "am equally pleased to assure you of my gratitude. Come and breakfast with us, my wife is still at her toilette. Come along."

I rose hastily, and just as I was leaving the room I saw the dreadful widow, who seemed full of glee, and said,—

"I thank you, sir; I thank you with all my heart. I beg to leave you at liberty again; I am going back to Soleure."

"Wait for a quarter of an hour, we are going to breakfast with Madame."

"I can't stop a moment, I have just wished her good day, and now I must be gone. Farewell, and remember me."

"Farewell, madam."

She had hardly gone before M.—— asked me if the woman was beside herself.

"One might think so, certainly," I replied, "for she has received nothing but politeness at my hands, and I think she might have waited to go back with you in the evening."

We went to breakfast and to discuss this abrupt leave-taking, and afterwards we took a turn in the garden where we found Madame Dubois. M.—— took possession of her; and as I thought his wife looking rather downcast I asked her if she had not slept well.

"I did not go to sleep till four o'clock this morning," she replied, "after vainly sitting up in bed waiting for you till that time. What unforeseen accident prevented your coming?"

I could not answer her question. I was petrified. I looked at her fixedly without replying; I could not shake off my astonishment. At last a dreadful suspicion came into my head that I had held within my arms for two hours the horrible monster whom I had foolishly received in my house. I was seized with a terrible tremor, which obliged me to go and take shelter behind the arbour and hide my emotion. I felt as though I should swoon away. I should certainly have fallen if I had not rested my head against a tree.

My first idea had been a fearful thought, which I hastened to repel, that Madame, having enjoyed me, wished to deny all knowledge of the fact—a device which is in the power of any woman who gives up her person in the dark to adopt, as it is impossible to convict her of lying. However, I knew the divine creature I had thought I possessed too well to believe her capable of such base deceit. I felt that she would have been lacking in delicacy, if she had said she had waited for me in vain by way of a jest; as in such a case as this the least doubt is a degradation. I was forced, then, to the conclusion that she had been supplanted by the infernal widow. How had she managed it? How had she ascertained our arrangements? I could not imagine, and I bewildered myself with painful surmises. Reason only comes to the aid of the mind when the confusion produced by painful thoughts has almost vanished. I concluded, then, that I had spent two hours with this abominable monster; and what increased my anguish, and made me loathe and despise myself still more, was that I could not help confessing that I had been perfectly happy. It was an unpardonable mistake, as the two women differed as much as white does from black, and though the darkness forbade my seeing, and the silence my hearing, my sense of touch should have enlightened me—after the first set-to, at all events, but my imagination was in a state of ecstasy. I cursed love, my nature, and above all the inconceivable weakness which had allowed me to receive into my house the serpent that had deprived me of an angel, and made me hate myself at the thought of having defiled myself with her. I resolved to die, after having torn to pieces with my own hands the monster who had made me so unhappy.

While I was strengthening myself in this resolution M.—— came up to me and asked me kindly if I were ill; he was alarmed to see me pale and covered with drops of sweat. "My wife," said the worthy man, "is uneasy about you, and sent me to look after you." I told him I had to leave her on account of a sudden dizziness, but that I began to feel better. "Let us rejoin her." Madame Dubois brought me a flask of strong waters, saying pleasantly that she was sure it was only the sudden departure of the widow that had put me out.

We continued our walk, and when we were far enough from the husband, who was with my housekeeper, I said I had been overcome by what she had said, but that it had doubtless been spoken jestingly.

"I was not jesting at all," said she, with a sigh, "tell me what prevented your coming."

Again I was struck dumb. I could not make up my mind to tell her the story, and I did not know what to say to justify myself. I was silent and confused when my housekeeper's little servant came up and gave me a letter which the wretched widow had sent her by an express. She had opened it, and found an enclosure addressed to me inside. I put it in my pocket, saying I would read it at my leisure. On Madame saying in joke that it was a love-letter, I could not laugh, and made no answer. The servant came to tell us that dinner was served, but I could touch nothing. My abstinence was put down to my being unwell.

I longed to read the letter, but I wished to be alone to do so, and that was a difficult matter to contrive.

Wishing to avoid the game of piquet which formed our usual afternoon's amusement, I took a cup of coffee, and said that I thought the fresh air would do me good. Madame seconded me, and guessing what I wanted she asked me to walk up and down with her in a sheltered alley in the garden. I offered her my arm, her husband offered his to my housekeeper, and we went out.

As soon as my mistress saw that we were free from observation, she spoke as follows,—

"I am sure that you spent the night with that malicious woman, and I am afraid of being compromised in consequence. Tell me everything; confide in me without reserve; 'tis my first intrigue, and if it is to serve as a lesson you should conceal nothing from me. I am sure you loved me once, tell me that you have not become my enemy."

"Good heavens! what are you saying? I your enemy!"

"Then tell me all, and before you read that wretched creature's letter. I adjure you in the name of love to hide nothing from me."

"Well, divine creature, I will do as you bid me. I came to your apartment at one o'clock, and as soon as I was in the second ante-chamber, I was taken by the arm, and a hand was placed upon my lips to impose silence; I thought I held you in my arms, and I laid you gently on the sofa. You must remember that I felt absolutely certain it was you; indeed, I can scarcely doubt it even now. I then passed with you, without a word being spoken, two of the most delicious hours I have ever experienced. Cursed hours! of which the remembrance will torment me for the remainder of my days. I left you at a quarter past three. The rest is known to you."

"Who can have told the monster that you were going to visit me at that hour?"

"I can't make out, and that perplexes me."

"You must confess that I am the most to be pitied of us three, and perhaps, alas! the only one who may have a just title to the name 'wretched.'"

"If you love me, in the name of Heaven do not say that; I have resolved to stab her, and to kill myself after having inflicted on her that punishment she so well deserves."

"Have you considered that the publicity of such an action would render me the most unfortunate of women? Let us be more moderate, sweetheart; you are not to blame for what has happened, and if possible I love you all the more. Give me the letter she has written to you. I will go away from you to read it, and you can read it afterwards, as if we were seen reading it together we should have to explain matters."

"Here it is."

I then rejoined her husband, whom my housekeeper was sending into fits of laughter. The conversation I had just had had calmed me a little, and the trustful way in which she had asked for the letter had done me good. I was in a fever to know the contents, and yet I dreaded to read it, as it could only increase my rage and I was afraid of the results.

Madame rejoined us, and after we had separated again she gave me the letter, telling me to keep it till I was alone. She asked me to give her my word of honour to do nothing without consulting her, and to communicate all my designs to her by means of her nurse.

"We need not fear the harpy saying anything about it," she remarked, "as she would first have to proclaim her own prostitution, and as for us, concealment is the best plan. And I would have you note that the horrible creature gives you a piece of advice you would do well to follow."

What completely tore my heart asunder during this interview was to see great tears—tears of love and grief—falling from her beautiful eyes; though to moderate my anguish she forced a smile. I knew too well the importance she attached to her fair fame not to guess that she was tormented with the idea that the terrible widow knew of the understanding between us, and the thought added fresh poignancy to my sorrow.

This amiable pair left me at seven in the evening, and I thanked the husband in such a manner that he could not doubt my sincerity, and, in truth, I said no more than I felt. There is no reason why the love one feels for a woman should hinder one from being the true friend of her husband—if she have a husband. The contrary view is a hateful prejudice, repugnant both to nature and to philosophy. After I had embraced him I was about to kiss the hand of his charming wife, but he begged me to embrace her too, which I did respectfully but feelingly.

I was impatient to read the terrible letter, and as soon as they were gone I shut myself up in my room to prevent any interruptions. The epistle was as follows:

"I leave your house, sir, well enough pleased, not that I have spent a couple of hours with you, for you are no better than any other man, but that I have revenged myself on the many open marks of contempt you have given me; for your private scorn I care little, and I willingly forgive you. I have avenged myself by unmasking your designs and the hypocrisy of your pretty prude, who will no longer be able to treat me with that irritating air of superiority which she, affecting a virtue which she does not possess, has displayed towards me. I have avenged myself in the fact that she must have been waiting for you all the night, and I would have given worlds to have heard the amusing conversation you must have had when she found out that I had taken for vengeance's sake, and not for love, the enjoyment which was meant for her. I have avenged myself because you can no longer pretend to think her a marvel of beauty, as having mistaken me for her, the difference between us must needs be slight; but I have done you a service, too, as the thought of what has happened should cure you of your passion. You will no longer adore her before all other women who are just as good as she. Thus I have disabused you, and you ought to feel grateful to me; but I dispense you from all gratitude, and do not care if you choose to hate me, provided your hatred leaves me in peace; but if I find your conduct objectionable in the future, I warn you that I will tell all, since I do not care for my own fame as I am a widow and mistress of my own actions. I need no man's favour, and care not what men may say of me. Your mistress, on the other hand, is in quite a different position.

"And here I will give you a piece of advice, which should convince you of my generosity. For the last ten years I have been troubled with a little ailment which has resisted all attempts at treatment. You exerted yourself to such an extent to prove how well you loved me that you must have caught the complaint. I advise you, then, to put yourself under treatment at once to weaken the force of the virus; but above all do not communicate it to your mistress, who might chance to hand it on to her husband and possibly to others, which would make a wretched woman of her, to my grief and sorrow, since she has never done me any harm. I felt certain that you two would deceive the worthy husband, and I wished to have proof; thus I made you take me in, and the position of the apartment you gave them was enough to remove all doubts; still I wanted to have proof positive. I had no need of any help to arrive at my ends, and I found it a pleasant joke to keep you in the dark. After passing two nights on the sofa all for nothing, I resolved on passing the third night there, and my perseverance was crowned with success. No one saw me, and my maid even is ignorant of my nocturnal wanderings, though in any case she is accustomed to observe silence. You are, then, at perfect liberty to bury the story in oblivion, and I advise you to do so.

"If you want a doctor, tell him to keep his counsel, for people at Soleure know of my little indisposition, and they might say you caught it from me, and this would do us both harm."

Her impudence struck me so gigantic in its dimensions that I almost laughed. I was perfectly aware that after the way I had treated her she must hate me, but I should not have thought she would have carried her perverse hatred so far. She had communicated to me an infectious disease, though I did not so far feel any symptoms; however, they would no doubt appear, and I sadly thought I should have to go away to be cured, to avoid the gossip of malicious wits. I gave myself up to reflection, and after two hours' thought I wisely resolved to hold my tongue, but to be revenged when the opportunity presented itself.

I had eaten nothing at dinner, and needed a good supper to make me sleep. I sat down to table with my housekeeper, but, like a man ashamed of himself, I dared not look her in the face.

CHAPTER XVI

Continuation of the Preceding Chapter—I Leave Soleure

When the servants had gone away and left us alone, it would have looked strange if we had remained as dumb as two posts; but in my state of mind I did not feel myself capable of breaking the silence. My dear Dubois, who began to love me because I made her happy, felt my melancholy react on herself, and tried to make me talk.

"Your sadness," said she, "is not like you; it frightens me. You may console yourself by telling me of your troubles, but do not imagine that my curiosity springs from any unworthy motive, I only want to be of service to you. You may rely on my being perfectly discreet; and to encourage you to speak freely, and to give you that trust in me which I think I deserve, I will tell you what I know and what I have learnt about yourself. My knowledge has not been obtained by any unworthy stratagems, or by a curiosity in affairs which do not concern me."

"I am pleased with what you say, my dear housekeeper. I see you are my friend, and I am grateful to you. Tell me all you know about the matter which is now troubling me, and conceal nothing."

"Very good. You are the lover and the beloved of Madame——. The widow whom you have treated badly has played you some trick which has involved you with your mistress, and then the wretched woman has 477 left your house with the most unpardonable rudeness this tortures you. You fear some disastrous consequences from which you cannot escape, your heart and mind are at war, and there is a struggle in your breast between passion and sentiment. Perhaps I am wrong, but yesterday you seemed to me happy and to-day miserable. I pity you, because you have inspired me with the tenderest feelings of friendship. I did my best to-day to converse with the husband that you might be free to talk to the wife, who seems to me well worthy of your love."

"All that you have said is true. Your friendship is dear to me, and I have a high opinion of your intellectual powers. The widow is a monster who has made me wretched in return for my contempt, and I cannot revenge myself on her. Honour will not allow me to tell you any more, and indeed it would be impossible for you or any one else to alleviate the grief that overwhelms me. It may possibly be my death, but in the mean time, my dear Dubois, I entreat you to continue your friendship towards me, and to treat me with entire candour. I shall always attend to what you say, and thus you will be of the greatest service to me. I shall not be ungrateful."

I spent a weary night as I had expected, for anger, the mother of vengeance, always made me sleepless, while sudden happiness had sometimes the same effect.

I rang for Le Duc early in the morning, but, instead of him, Madame Dubois's ugly little attendant came, and told me that my man was ill, and that the housekeeper would bring me my chocolate. She came in directly after, and I had no sooner swallowed the chocolate than I was seized with a violent attack of sickness, the effect of anger, which at its height may kill the man who cannot satisfy it. My concentrated rage called for vengeance on the dreadful widow, the chocolate came on the top of the anger, and if it had not been rejected I should have been killed; as it was I was quite exhausted. Looking at my housekeeper I saw she was in tears, and asked her why she wept.

"Good heavens! Do you think I have a heart of stone?"

"Calm yourself; I see you pity me. Leave me, and I hope I shall be able to get some sleep."

I went to sleep soon after, and I did not wake till I had slept for seven hours. I felt restored to life. I rang the bell, my housekeeper came in, and told me the surgeon of the place had called. She looked very melancholy, but on seeing my more cheerful aspect I saw gladness reappearing on her pretty face.

"We will dine together, dearest," said I, "but tell the surgeon to come in. I want to know what he has to say to me."

The worthy man entered, and after looking carefully round the room to see that we were alone, he came up to me, and whispered in my ear that Le Duc had a malady of a shameful character.

I burst out laughing, as I had been expecting some terrible news.

"My dear doctor," said I, "do all you can to cure him, and I will pay you handsomely, but next time don't look so doleful when you have anything to tell me. How old are you?"

"Nearly eighty."

"May God help you!"

I was all the more ready to sympathize with my poor Spaniard, as I expected to find myself in a like case.

What a fellow-feeling there is between the unfortunate! The poor man will seek in vain for true compassion at the rich man's doors; what he receives is a sacrifice to ostentation and not true benevolence; and the man in sorrow should not look for pity from one to whom sorrow is unknown, if there be such a person on the earth.

My housekeeper came in to dress me, and asked me what had been the doctor's business.

"He must have said something amusing to make you laugh."

"Yes, and I should like to tell you what it was; but before I do so I must ask you if you know what the venereal disease is?"

"Yes, I do; Lady Montagu's footman died of it while I was with her."

"Very good, but you should pretend not to know what it is, and imitate other ladies who assume an ignorance which well becomes them. Poor Le Duc has got this disease."

"Poor fellow, I am sorry for him! Were you laughing at that?"

"No; it was the air of mystery assumed by the old doctor which amused me."

"I too have a confidence to make, and when you have heard it you must either forgive me or send me away directly."

"Here is another bother. What the devil can you have done? Quick! tell me."

"Sir, I have robbed you!"

"What robbed me? When? How? Can you return me what you have taken? I should not have thought you capable of such a thing. I never forgive a robber or a liar."

"You are too hasty, sir. I am sure you will forgive me, as I robbed you only half an hour ago, and I am now going to return to you the theft."

"You are a singular woman, my dear. Come, I will vouchsafe full forgiveness, but restore immediately what you have taken."

"This is what I stole."

"What! that monster's letter? Did you read it?"

"Yes, of course, for otherwise I should not have committed a theft, should I?"

"You have robbed me my secret, then, and that is a thing you cannot give me back. You have done very wrong."

"I confess I have. My theft is all the greater in that I cannot make restoration. Nevertheless, I promise never to speak a word of it all my life, and that ought to gain me my pardon. Give it me quickly."

"You are a little witch. I forgive you, and here is the pledge of my mercy." So saying I fastened my lips on hers.

"I don't doubt the validity of your pardon; you have signed with a double and a triple seal."

"Yes; but for the future do not read, or so much as touch, any of my papers, as I am the depositary of secrets of which I am not free to dispose."

"Very good; but what shall I do when I find papers on the ground, as that letter was?"

"You must pick them up, but not read them."

"I promise to do so."

"Very well, my dear; but you must forget the horrors you have read."

"Listen to me. Allow me to remember what I have read; perhaps you may be the gainer. Let us talk over this affair, which has made my hair stand on end. This monster of immodesty has given you two mortal blows—one in the body and one in the soul; but that is not the worst, as she thinks that Madame's honour is in her keeping. This, in my thinking, is the worst of all; for, in spite of the affront, your mutual love might continue, and the disease which the infamous creature has communicated to you would pass off; but if the malicious woman carries out her threats, the honour of your charming mistress is gone beyond return. Do not try to make me forget the matter, then, but let us talk it over and see what can be done."

I thought I was dreaming when I heard a young woman in her position reasoning with more acuteness than Minerva displays in her colloquies with Telemachus. She had captured not only my esteem but my respect.

"Yes, my dear," I answered, "let us think over some plan for delivering a woman who deserves the respect of all good men from this imminent danger; and the very thought that we have some chance of success makes me indebted to you. Let us think of it and talk of it from noon to night. Think kindly of Madame——, pardon her first slip, protect her honour, and have pity on my distress. From henceforth call me no more your master but your friend. I will be your friend till death; I swear it to you. What you say is full of wisdom; my heart is yours. Embrace me."

"No, no, that is not necessary; we are young people, and we might perhaps allow ourselves to go astray. I only wish for your friendship; but I do not want you to give it to me for nothing. I wish to deserve it by giving you solid proofs of my friendship for you. In the meanwhile I will tell them to serve dinner, and I hope that after you have eaten something you will be quite well."

I was astonished at her sagacity. It might all be calculated artifice, and her aim might be to seduce me, but I did not trouble myself about that. I found myself almost in love with her, and like to be the dupe of her principles, which would have made themselves felt, even if she had openly shared my love. I decided that I would add no fuel to my flames, and felt certain that they would go out of their own accord. By leaving my love thus desolate it would die of exhaustion. I argued like a fool. I forgot that it is not possible to stop at friendship with a pretty woman whom one sees constantly, and especially when one suspects her of being in love herself. At its height friendship becomes love, and the palliative one is forced to apply to soothe it for a moment only increases its intensity. Such was the experience of Anacreon with Smerdis, and Cleobulus with Badyllus. A Platonist who pretends that one is able to live with a young woman of whom one is fond, without becoming more than her friend, is a visionary who knows not what he says. My housekeeper was too young, too pretty, and above all too pleasant, she had too keen a wit, for me not to be captivated by all these qualities conjoined; I was bound to become her lover.

We dined quietly together without saying anything about the affair we had at heart, for nothing is more imprudent or more dangerous than to speak in the presence of servants, who out of maliciousness or ignorance put the worst construction on what they hear; add or diminish, and think themselves privileged to divulge their master's secrets, especially as they know them without having been entrusted with them.

As soon as we were alone, my dear Dubois asked me if I had sufficient proof of Le Duc's fidelity.

"Well, my dear, he is a rascal and a profligate, full of impudence, sharp-witted, ignorant, a fearful liar, and nobody but myself has any power over him. However, he has one good quality, and that is blind obedience to my orders. He defies the stick, and he would defy the gallows if it were far enough off. When I have to ford a river on my travels, he strips off his clothes without my telling him, and jumps in to see if I can across in safety."

"That will do; he is just what we want under the circumstances. I will begin by assuring you, my dear friend, as you will have me style you thus, that Madame's honour is perfectly safe. Follow my advice, and if the detestable widow does not take care she will be the only person put to shame. But we want Le Duc; without him we can do nothing. Above all we must find out how he contracted his disease, as several circumstances might throw obstacles in the way of my design. Go to him at once and find out all particulars, and if he has told any of the servants what is the matter with him. When you have heard what he has to say, warn him to keep the matter quiet."

I made no objection, and without endeavouring to penetrate her design I went to Le Duc. I found him lying on his bed by himself. I sat down beside him with a smile on my face, and promised to have him cured if he would tell me all the circumstances of the case.

"With all my heart, sir, the matter happened like this. The day you sent me to Soleure to get your letters, I got down at a roadside dairy to get a glass of milk. It was served to me by a young wench who caught my fancy, and I gave her a hug; she raised no objection, and in a quarter of an hour she made me what you see."

"Have you told anyone about it?"

"I took good care not to do so, as I should only have got laughed at. The doctor is the only one who knows what is the matter, and he tells me the swelling will be gone down before tomorrow, and I hope I shall be able by that time to wait upon you."

"Very good, but remember to keep your own counsel."

I proceeded to inform my Minerva of our conversation, and she said,—

"Tell me whether the widow could take her oath that she had spent the two hours on the sofa with you."

"No, for she didn't see me, and I did not say a word."

"Very good; then sit down at your desk and write, and tell her she is a liar, as you did not leave your room at all, and that you are making the necessary enquiries in your household to find out who is the wretched person she has unwittingly contaminated. Write at once and send off your letter directly. In an hour and a half's time you can write another letter; or rather you can copy what I am just going to put down."

"My dear, I see your plan; it is an ingenious one, but I have given my word of honour to Madame to take no steps in the matter without first consulting her."

"Then your word of honour must give way to the necessity of saving her honour. Your love retards your steps, but everything depends on our promptitude, and on the interval between the first and second letter. Follow my advice, I beg of you, and you will know the rest from the letter I am going to write for you to copy. Quick I write letter number one."

I did not allow myself to reflect. I was persuaded that no better plan could be found than that of my charming governess, and I proceeded to write the following love-letter to the impudent monster:

"The impudence of your letter is in perfect accord with the three nights you spent in discovering a fact which has no existence save in your own perverse imagination. Know, cursed woman, that I never left my room, and that I have not to deplore the shame of having passed two hours with a being such as you. God knows with whom you did pass them, but I mean to find out if the whole story is not the creation of your devilish brain, and when I do so I will inform you.

"You may thank Heaven that I did not open your letter till after M. and Madame had gone. I received it in their presence, but despising the hand that wrote it I put it in my pocket, little caring what infamous stuff it contained. If I had been curious enough to read it and my guests had seen it, I would have you know that I would have gone in pursuit of you, and at this moment you would have been a corpse. I am quite well, and have no symptoms of any complaint, but I shall not lower myself to convince you of my health, as your eyes would carry contagion as well as your wretched carcase."

I shewed the letter to my dear Dubois, who thought it rather strongly expressed, but approved of it on the whole; I then sent it to the horrible being who had caused me such unhappiness. An hour and a half afterwards I sent her the following letter, which I copied without addition or subtraction:

"A quarter of an hour after I had sent off my letter, the village doctor came to tell me that my man had need of his treatment for a disease of a shameful nature which he had contracted quite recently. I told him to take care of his patient; and when he had gone I went to see the invalid, who confessed, after some pressure, that he had received this pretty present from you. I asked him how he had contrived to obtain access to you, and he said that he saw you going by your self in the dark into the apartment of M.——. Knowing that I had gone to bed, and having no further services to render me, curiosity made him go and see what you were doing there by stealth, as if you had wanted to see the lady, who would be in bed by that time, you would not have gone by the door leading to the garden. He at first thought that you went there with ill-intent, and he waited an hour to see if you stole anything, in which case he would have arrested you; but as you did not come out, and he heard no noise, he resolved to go in after you, and found you had left the door open. He has assured me that he had no intentions in the way of carnal enjoyment, and I can well believe him. He tells me he was on the point of crying for help, when you took hold of him and put your hand over his mouth; but he changed his plans on finding himself drawn gently to a couch and covered with kisses. You plainly took him for somebody else, 'and,' said he, 'I did her a service which she has done ill to recompense in this fashion.' He left you without saying a word as soon as the day began to dawn, his motive being fear of recognition. It is easy to see that you took my servant for myself, for in the night, you know, all cats are grey, and I congratulate you on obtaining an enjoyment you certainly would not have had from me, as I should most surely have recognized you directly from your breath and your aged charms, and I can tell you it would have gone hard with you. Luckily for you and for me, things happened otherwise. I may tell you that the poor fellow is furious, and intends making you a visit, from which course I believe I have no right to dissuade him. I advise you to hear him politely, and to be in a generous mood when he comes, as he is a determined fellow like all Spaniards, and if you do not treat him properly he will publish the matter, and you will have to take the consequences. He will tell you himself what his terms are, and I daresay you will be wise enough to grant them."

An hour after I had sent off this epistle I received a reply to my first letter. She told me that my device was an ingenious one, but that it was no good, as she knew what she was talking about. She defied me to shew her that I was healthy in the course of a few days.

While we were at supper, my dear Dubois tried her utmost to cheer me up, but all to no purpose; I was too much under the influence of strong emotion to yield to her high spirits. We discussed the third step, which would put an apex to the scheme and cover the impudent woman with shame. As I had written the two letters according to my housekeeper's instructions, I determined to follow her advice to the end. She told me what to say to Le Duc in the morning; and she was curious to know what sort of stuff he was made of, she begged me to let her listen behind the curtains of my bed.

Next morning Le Due came in, and I asked if he could ride on horseback to Soleure.

"Yes, sir," he replied, "but the doctor tells me I must begin to bathe to-morrow."

"Very good. As soon as your horse is ready, set out and go to Madame F——, but do not let her know you come from me, or suspect that you are a mere emissary of mine. Say that you want to speak to her. If she refuses to receive you, wait outside in the street; but I fancy she will receive you, and without a witness either. Then say to her, 'You have given me my complaint without having been asked, and I require you to give me sufficient money to get myself cured.' Add that she made you work for two hours in the dark, and that if it had not been for the fatal present she had given to you, you would have said nothing about it; but that finding yourself in such a state (you needn't be ashamed to shew her) she ought not to be astonished at your taking such a course. If she resists, threaten her with the law. That's all you have to do, but don't let my name appear. Return directly without loss of time, that I may know how you have got on."

"That's all very fine, sir, but if this jolly wench has me pitched out of window, I shan't come home quite so speedily."

"Quite so, but you needn't be afraid; I will answer for your safety."

"It's a queer business you are sending me on."

"You are the only man I would trust to do it properly."

"I will do it all right, but I want to ask you one or two essential questions. Has the lady really got the what d'you call it?"

"She has."

"I am sorry for her. But how am I to stick to it that she has peppered me, when I have never spoken to her?"

"Do you usually catch that complaint by speaking, booby?"

"No, but one speaks in order to catch it, or while one is catching it."

"You spent two hours in the dark with her without a word being spoken, and she will see that she gave this fine present to you while she thought she was giving it to another."

"Ah! I begin to see my way, sir. But if we were in the dark, how was I to know it was she I had to do with?

"Thus: you saw her going in by the garden door, and you marked her unobserved. But you may be sure she won't ask you any of these questions."

"I know what to do now. I will start at once, and I am as curious as you to know what her answer will be. But here's another question comes into my head. She may try to strike a bargain over the sum I am to ask for my cure; if so, shall I be content with three hundred francs?"

"That's too much for her, take half."

"But it isn't much for two hours of such pleasure for her and six weeks of such pain for me."

"I will make up the rest to you."

"That's good hearing. She is going to pay for damage she has done. I fancy I see it all, but I shall say nothing. I would bet it is you to whom she has made this fine present, and that you want to pay her out."

"Perhaps so; but keep your own counsel and set out."

"Do you know I think the rascal is unique," said my dear Dubois, emerging from her hiding-place, "I had hard work to keep from laughing when he said that if he were pitched out of the window he would not come back so soon. I am sure he will acquit himself better than ever did diplomatist. When he gets to Soleure the monster will have already dispatched her reply to your second letter. I am curious to see how it will turn out."

"To you, my dear, the honour of this comedy belongs. You have conducted this intrigue like a past master in the craft. It could never be taken for the work of a novice."

"Nevertheless, it is my first and I hope it will be my last intrigue."

"I hope she won't defy me to 'give evidence of my health'."

"You are quite well so far, I think?"

"Yes; and, by the way, it is possible she may only have leucorrhoea. I am longing to see the end of the piece, and to set my mind at rest."

"Will you give Madame an account of our scheme?"

"Yes; but I shall not be able to give you the credit you deserve."

"I only want to have credit in your eyes."

"You cannot doubt that I honour you immensely, and I shall certainly not deprive you of the reward that is your due."

"The only reward I ask for is for you to be perfectly open with me."

"You are very wonderful. Why do you interest yourself so much in my affairs? I don't like to think you are really inquisitive."

"You would be wrong to think that I have a defect which would lower me in my own eyes. Be sure, sir, that I shall only be curious when you are sad."

"But what can have made you feel so generously towards me?"

"Only your honourable conduct towards me."

"You touch me profoundly, and I promise to confide in you for the future."

"You will make me happy."

Le Duc had scarcely gone an hour when a messenger on foot came to bring me a second letter from the widow. He also gave me a small packet, telling me that he had orders to wait for a reply. I sent him down to wait, and I gave the letter to Madame Dubois, that she might see what it contained. While she was reading it I leant upon the window, my heart beating violently.

"Everything is getting on famously," cried my housekeeper. "Here is the letter; read it."

"Whether I am being told the truth, or whether I am the victim of a myth arising from your fertile imagination (for which you are too well known all over Europe), I will regard the whole story as being true, as I am not in a position to disprove it. I am deeply grieved to have injured an innocent man who has never done me any ill, and I will willingly pay the penalty by giving him a sum which will be more than sufficient to cure him of the plague with which I infected him. I beg that you will give him the twenty-five louis I am sending you; they will serve to restore him to health, and to make him forget the bitterness of the pleasure I am so sorry to have procured for him. And now are you sufficiently generous to employ your authority as master to enjoin on your man the most absolute secrecy? I hope so, for you have reason to dread my vengeance otherwise. Consider that, if this affair is allowed to transpire, it will be easy for me to give it a turn which may be far from pleasant to you, and which will force the worthy man you are deceiving to open his eyes; for I have not changed my opinion, as I have too many proofs of your understanding with his wife. As I do not desire that we should meet again, I shall go to Lucerne on the pretext of family concerns. Let me know that you have got this letter."

"I am sorry," I said, "to have sent Le Duc, as the harpy is violent, and
I am afraid of something happening to him."

"Don't be afraid," she replied, "nothing will happen, and it is better that they should see each other; it makes it more certain. Send her the money directly; she will have to give it to him herself, and your vengeance will be complete. She will not be able to entertain the slightest suspicion, especially if Le Duc shews her her work, and in two or three hours you will have the pleasure of hearing everything from his lips. You have reason to bless your stars, as the honour of the woman you love is safe. The only thing that can trouble you is the remembrance of the widow's foul embraces, and the certainty that the prostitute has communicated her complaint to you. Nevertheless, I hope it may prove a slight attack and be easily cured. An inveterate leucorrhoea is not exactly a venereal disease, and I have heard people in London say that it was rarely contagious. We ought to be very thankful that she is going to Lucerne. Laugh and be thankful; there is certainly a comic touch in our drama."

"Unfortunately, it is tragi-comic. I know the human heart, and I am sure that I must have forfeited Madame's affections."

"It is true that——; but this is not the time to be thinking of such matters. Quick! write to her briefly and return her the twenty-five Louis."

My reply was as follows:

"Your unworthy suspicions, your abominable design of revenge, and the impudent letter you wrote me, are the only causes of your no doubt bitter repentance. I hope that it will restore peace to your conscience. Our messengers have crossed, through no fault of mine. I send you the twenty-five Louis; you can give them to the man yourself. I could not prevent my servant from paying you a visit, but this time you will not keep him two hours, and you will not find it difficult to appease his anger. I wish you a good journey, and I shall certainly flee all occasions of meeting you, for I always avoid the horrible; and you must know, odious woman, that it isn't everybody who endeavours to ruin the reputation of their friends. If you see the apostolic nuncio at Lucerne, ask him about me, and he will tell you what sort of a reputation I have in Europe. I can assure you that Le Duc has only spoken to me of his misadventure, and that if you treat him well he will be discreet, as he certainly has nothing to boast of. Farewell."

My dear Minerva approved of this letter, and I sent it with the money by the messenger.

"The piece is not yet done," said my housekeeper, "we have three scenes more:"

"What are they?"

"The return of your Spaniard, the appearance of the disease, and the astonishment of Madame when she hears it all."

I counted the moments for Le Duc to return, but in vain; he did not appear. I was in a state of great anxiety, although my dear Dubois kept telling me that the only reason he was away so long was that the widow was out. Some people are so happily constituted that they never admit the possibility of misfortune. I was like that myself till the age of thirty, when I was put under the Leads. Now I am getting into my dotage and look on the dark side of everything. I am invited to a wedding, and see nought but gloom; and witnessing the coronation of Leopold, at Prague, I say to myself, 'Nolo coronari'. Cursed old age, thou art only worthy of dwelling in hell, as others before me have thought also, 'tristisque senectus'.

About half-past nine my housekeeper looked out, and saw Le Duc by the moonlight coming along at a good pace. That news revived me. I had no light in the room, and my housekeeper ran to hide in the recess, for she would not have missed a word of the Spaniard's communication.

"I am dying of hunger," said he, as he came in. "I had to wait for that woman till half-past six. When she came in she found me on the stairs and told me to go about my business, as she had nothing to say to me.

"'That may be, fair lady,' I replied; 'but I have a few words to say to you, and I have been waiting here for a cursed time with that intent.'

"'Wait a minute,' she replied; and then putting into her pocket a packet and a letter which I thought was addressed in your writing, she told me to follow her. As soon as I got to her room, I saw there was no one else present, and I told her that she had infected me, and that I wanted the wherewithal to pay the doctor. As she said nothing I proceeded to convince her of my infected state, but she turned away her head, and said,—

"'Have you been waiting for me long?

"'Since eleven, without having had a bite or a sup.'

"Thereupon she went out, and after asking the servant, whom I suppose she had sent here, what time he had come back, she returned to me, shut the door, and gave me the packet, telling me that it contained twenty-five Louis for my cure, and that if I valued my life I would keep silence in the matter. I promised to be discreet, and with that I left here, and here I am.

"Does the packet belong to me?"

"Certainly. Have some supper and go to bed."

My dear Dubois came out of her recess and embraced me, and we spent a happy evening. Next morning I noticed the first symptoms of the disease the hateful widow had communicated to me, but in three or four days I found it was of a very harmless character, and a week later I was quite rid of it. My poor Spaniard, on the other hand, was in a pitiable case.

I passed the whole of the next morning in writing to Madame. I told her circumstantially all I had done, in spite of my promise to consult her, and I sent her copies of all the letters to convince her that our enemy had gone to Lucerne with the idea that her vengeance had been only an imaginary one. Thus I shewed her that her honour was perfectly safe. I ended by telling her that I had noticed the first symptoms of the disease, but that I was certain of getting rid of it in a very few days. I sent my letter through her nurse, and in two days' time I had a few lines from her informing me that I should see her in the course of the week in company with her husband and M. de Chavigni.

Unhappy !! I was obliged to renounce all thoughts of love, but my Dubois, who was with me nearly all day on account of Le Duc's illness, began to stand me in good stead. The more I determined to be only a friend to her, the more I was taken with her; and it was in vain that I told myself that from seeing her without any love-making my sentiment for her would die a natural death. I had made her a present of a ring, telling her that whenever she wanted to get rid of it I would give her a hundred louis for it; but this could only happen in time of need—an impossible contingency while she continued with me, and I had no idea of sending her away. She was natural and sincere, endowed with a ready wit and good reasoning powers. She had never been in love, and she had only married to please Lady Montagu. She only wrote to her mother, and to please her I read the letters. They were full of filial piety, and were admirably written.

One day the fancy took me to ask to read the letters her mother wrote in reply. "She never replies," said she, "For an excellent reason, namely, that she cannot write. I thought she was dead when I came back from England, and it was a happy surprise to find her in perfect health when I got to Lausanne."

"Who came with you from England?"

"Nobody."

"I can't credit that. Young, beautiful, well dressed, obliged to associate casually with all kinds of people, young men and profligates (for there are such everywhere), how did you manage to defend yourself?"

"Defend myself? I never needed to do so. The best plan for a young woman is never to stare at any man, to pretend not to hear certain questions and certainly not to answer them, to sleep by herself in a room where there is a lock and key, or with the landlady when possible. When a girl has travelling adventures, one may safely say that she has courted them, for it is easy to be discreet in all countries if one wishes."

She spoke justly. She assured me that she had never had an adventure and had never tripped, as she was fortunate enough not to be of an amorous disposition. Her naïve stories, her freedom from prudery, and her sallies full of wit and good sense, amused me from morning till night, and we sometimes thoued each other; this was going rather far, and should have shewn us that we were on the brink of the precipice. She talked with much admiration of the charms of Madame, and shewed the liveliest interest in my stories of amorous adventure. When I got on risky ground, I would make as if I would fain spare her all unseemly details, but she begged me so gracefully to hide nothing, that I found myself obliged to satisfy her; but when my descriptions became so faithful as almost to set us on fire, she would burst into a laugh, put her hand over my mouth, and fly like a hunted gazelle to her room, and then lock herself in. One day I asked her why she did so, and she answered, "To hinder you from coming to ask me for what I could not refuse you at such moments."

The day before that on which M. and Madame and M. de Chavigni came to dine with me, she asked me if I had had any amorous adventures in Holland. I told her about Esther, and when I came to the mole and my inspection of it, my charming curiosity ran to stop my mouth, her sides shaking with laughter. I held her gently to me, and could not help seeking whether she had a mole in the same place, to which she opposed but a feeble resistance. I was prevented by my unfortunate condition from immolating the victim on the altar of love, so we confined ourselves to a make-believe combat which only lasted a minute; however, our eyes took in it, and our excited feelings were by no means appeased. When we had done she said, laughing, but yet discreetly,—

"My dear friend, we are in love with one another; and if we do not take care we shall not long be content with this trifling."

Sighing as she spoke, she wished me good night and went to bed with her ugly little maid. This was the first time we had allowed ourselves to be overcome by the violence of our passion, but the first step was taken. As I retired to rest I felt that I was in love, and foresaw that I should soon be under the rule of my charming housekeeper.

M. and Madame—and M. Chavigni gave us an agreeable surprise, the next day, by coming to dine with us, and we passed the time till dinner by walking in the garden. My dear Dubois did the honours of the table, and I was glad to see that my two male guests were delighted with her, for they did not leave her for a moment during the afternoon, and I was thus enabled to tell my charmer all I had written to her. Nevertheless I took care not to say a word about the share my housekeeper had had in the matter, for my mistress would have been mortified at the thought that her weakness was known to her.

"I was delighted to read your letters," said she, "and to hear that that villainous woman can no longer flatter herself upon having spent two hours with you. But tell me, how can you have actually spent them with her without noticing, in spite of the dark, the difference between her and me? She is much shorter, much thinner, and ten years older. Besides, her breath is disagreeable, and I think you know that I have not that defect. Certainly, you could not see her hair, but you could touch, and yet you noticed nothing! I can scarcely believe it!"

"Unhappily, it is only too true. I was inebriated with love, and thinking only of you, I saw nothing but you."

"I understand how strong the imagination would be at first, but this element should have been much diminished after the first or second assault; and, above all, because she differs from me in a matter which I cannot conceal and she cannot supply."

"You are right—a burst of Venus! When I think that I only touched two dangling flabby breasts, I feel as if I did not deserve to live!"

"And you felt them, and they did not disgust you!"

"Could I be disgusted, could I even reflect, when I felt certain that I held you in my arms, you for whom I would give my life. No, a rough skin, a stinking breath, and a fortification carried with far too much ease; nothing could moderate my amorous fury."

"What do I hear? Accursed and unclean woman, nest of impurities! And could you forgive me all these defects?"

"I repeat, the idea that I possessed you deprived me of my thinking faculties; all seemed to me divine."

"You should have treated me like a common prostitute, you should even have beaten me on finding me such as you describe."

"Ah! now you are unjust!"

"That may be; I am so enraged against that monster that my anger deprives me of reason. But now that she thinks that she had to do with a servant, and after the degrading visit she has had she ought to die of rage and shame. What astonishes me is her believing it, for he is shorter than you by four inches. And how can she imagine that a servant would do it as well as you? It's not likely. I am sure she is in love with him now. Twenty-five louis! He would have been content with ten. What a good thing that the poor fellow's illness happened so conveniently. But I suppose you had to tell him all?"

"Not at all. I gave him to understand that she had made an appointment with me in that room, and that I had really spent two hours with her, not speaking for fear of being heard. Then, thinking over the orders I gave him, he came to the conclusion that on finding myself diseased afterwards I was disgusted, and being able to disavow my presence I had done so for the sake of revenge."

"That's admirable, and the impudence of the Spaniard passes all belief. But her impudence is the most astonishing thing of all. But supposing her illness had been a mere trick to frighten you, what a risk the rascal would have run!"

"I was afraid of that, as I had no symptoms of disease whatever."

"But now you really have it, and all through my fault. I am in despair."

"Be calm, my angel, my disease is of a very trifling nature. I am only taking nitre, and in a week I shall be quite well again. I hope that then . . . ."

"Ah! my dear friend."

"What?"

"Don't let us think of that any more, I beseech you."

"You are disgusted, and not unnaturally; but your love cannot be very strong, Ah! how unhappy I am."

"I am more unhappy than you. I love you, and you would be thankless indeed if you ceased to love me. Let us love each other, but let us not endeavour to give one another proofs of our love. It might be fatal. That accursed widow! She is gone away, and in a fortnight we shall be going also to Bale, where we remain till the end of November."

The die is cast, and I see that I must submit to your decision, or rather to my destiny, for none but fatal events have befallen me since I came to Switzerland. My only consoling thought is that I have made your honour safe."

"You have won my husband's friendship and esteem; we shall always be good friends."

"If you are going I feel that I must go before you. That will tend to convince the wretched author of my woe that there is nothing blame-worthy in my friendship for you."

"You reason like an angel, and you convince me more and more of your love. Where are you going?"

"To Italy; but I shall take Berne and Geneva on my way."

"You will not be coming to Bale, then? I am glad to hear it, in spite of the pleasure it would give me to see you. No doubt your arrival would give a handle for the gossips, and I might suffer by it. But if possible, in the few days you are to remain, shew yourself to be in good spirits, for sadness does not become you."

We rejoined the ambassador and M.—— who had not had time to think about us, as my dear Dubois had kept them amused by her lively conversation. I reproached her for the way in which she husbanded her wit as far as I was concerned, and M. de Chavigni, seizing the opportunity, told us it was because we were in love, and lovers are known to be chary of their words. My housekeeper was not long in finding a repartee, and she again began to entertain the two gentlemen, so that I was enabled to continue my walk with Madame, who said,—

"Your housekeeper, my dear friend, is a masterpiece. Tell me the truth, and I promise to give you a mark of my gratitude that will please you before I go."

"Speak; what do you wish to know?"

"You love her and she loves you in return."

"I think you are right, but so far . . . ."

"I don't want to know any more, for if matters are not yet arranged they soon will be, and so it comes to the same thing. If you had told me you did not love her I should not have believed you, for I can't conceive that a man of your age can live with a woman like that without loving her. She is very pretty and exceedingly intelligent, she has good spirits, talents, an excellent manner, and she speaks exceedingly well: that is enough to charm you, and I expect you will find it difficult to separate from her. Lebel did her a bad turn in sending her to you, as she used to have an excellent reputation, and now she will no longer be able to get a place with ladies in the highest society."

"I shall take her to Berne."

"That is a good idea."

Just as they were going I said that I should soon be coming to Soleure to thank them for the distinguished reception they had given me, as I proposed leaving in a few days. The idea of never seeing Madame again was so painful to me that as soon as I got in I went to bed, and my housekeeper, respecting my melancholy, retired after wishing me good-night.

In two or three days I received a note from my charmer, bidding me call upon them the day following at about ten o'clock, and telling me I was to ask for dinner. I carried out her orders to the letter. M. gave me a most friendly reception, but saying that he was obliged to go into the country and could not be home till one o'clock, he begged me not to be offended if he delivered me over to his wife for the morning. Such is the fate of a miserable husband! His wife was engaged with a young girl at tambour-work; I accepted her company on the condition that she would not allow me to disturb her work.

The girl went away at noon, and soon after we went to enjoy the fresh air outside the house. We sat in a summer-house from which, ourselves unseen, we could see all the carriages that approached the house.

"Why, dearest, did you not procure me the bliss when I was in good health."

"Because at that time my husband suspected that you turned yourself into a waiter for my sake, and that you could not be indifferent towards me. Your discretion has destroyed his suspicions; and also your housekeeper, whom he believes to be your wife, and who has taken his fancy to such an extent, that I believe he would willingly consent to an exchange, for a few days at any rate. Would you agree?"

"Ah! if the exchange could be effected."

Having only an hour before me, and foreseeing that it would be the last I should pass beside her, I threw myself at her feet. She was full of affection, and put no obstacles in the way of my desires, save those which my own feelings dictated, for I loved her too well to consent to injure her health. I did all I could to replace the utmost bliss, but the pleasure she enjoyed doubtless consisted in a great measure in shewing me her superiority to the horrible widow.

When we saw the husband's carriage coming, we rose and took care that the worthy man should not find us in the arbour. He made a thousand excuses for not having returned sooner.

We had an excellent dinner, and at table he talked almost entirely of my housekeeper, and he seemed moved when I said I meant to take her to Lausanne to her mother. I took leave of them at five o'clock with a broken heart, and from there I went to M. de Chavigni and told him all my adventures. He had a right to be told, as he had done all in his power to insure the success of a project which had only failed by an unexampled fatality.

In admiration of my dear Dubois's wit—for I did not conceal the part she played he said that old as he was he should think himself quite happy if he had such a woman with him, and he was much pleased when I told him that I was in love with her. "Don't give yourself the trouble, my dear Casanova, of running from house to house to take leave," said the amiable nobleman. "It can be done just as well at the assembly, and you need not even stay to supper, if you don't want to."

I followed his advice, and thus saw again Madame as I thought, for the last time, but I was wrong; I saw her ten years afterwards; and at the proper time the reader will see where, when, how, and under what circumstances.

Before going away, I followed the ambassador to his room to thank him as he deserved, for his kindness, and to ask him to give me a letter of introduction for Berne, where I thought of staying a fortnight. I also begged him to send Lebel to me that we might settle our accounts. He told me that Lebel should bring me a letter for M. de Muralt, the Mayor of Thun.

When I got home, feeling sad on this, the eve of my leaving a town where I had but trifling victories and heavy losses, I thanked my housekeeper for waiting for me, and to give her a good night I told her that in three days we should set out for Berne, and that my mails must be packed.

Next day, after a somewhat silent breakfast, she said,—

"You will take me with you, won't you?"

"Certainly, if you like me well enough to want to go."

"I would go with you to the end of the world, all the more as you are now sick and sad, and when I saw you first you were blithe and well. If I must leave you, I hope at least to see you happy first."

The doctor came in just then to tell me that my poor Spaniard was so ill that he could not leave his bed.

"I will have him cured at Berne," said I; "tell him that we are going to dine there the day after to-morrow."

"I must tell you, sir, that though it's only a seven leagues' journey, he cannot possibly undertake it as he has lost the use of all his limbs."

"I am sorry to hear that, doctor."

"I dare say, but it's true."

"I must verify the matter with my own eyes;" and so saying I went to see Le Duc.

I found the poor rascal, as the doctor had said, incapable of motion. He had only the use of his tongue and his eyes.

"You are in a pretty state," said I to him.

"I am very ill, sir, though otherwise I feel quite well."

"I expect so, but as it is you can't move, and I want to dine at Berne the day after to-morrow."

"Have me carried there, I shall get cured."

"You are right, I will have you carried in a litter."

"I shall look like a saint out for a walk."

I told one of the servants to look after him, and to see to all that was necessary for our departure. I had him taken to the "Falcon" by two horses who drew his litter.

Lebel came at noon and gave me the letter his master had written for M. de Murat. He brought his receipts and I paid everything without objection, as I found him an entirely honest man, and I had him to dinner with Madame Dubois and myself. I did not feel disposed to talk, and I was glad to see that they got on without me; they talked away admirably and amused me, for Lebel was by no means wanting in wit. He said he was very glad I had given him an opportunity of knowing the housekeeper, as he could not say he had known her before, having only seen her two or three times in passing through Lausanne. On rising from the table he asked my permission to write to her, and she, putting in her voice, called on him not to forget to do so.

Lebel was a good-natured man, of an honest appearance, and approaching his fiftieth year. Just as he was going, without asking my leave, he embraced her in the French fashion, and she seemed not to have the slightest objection.

She told me as soon as he was gone that this worthy man might be useful to her, and that she was delighted to enter into a correspondence with him.

The next day was spent in putting everything in order for our short journey, and Le Duc went off in his litter, intending to rest for the night at four leagues from Soleure. On the day following, after I had remembered the door-keeper, the cook, and the man-servant I was leaving behind, I set out in my carriage with the charming Dubois, and at eleven o'clock I arrived at the inn at Berne, where Le Duc had preceded me by two hours. In the first place, knowing the habits of Swiss innkeepers, I made an agreement with the landlord; and I then told the servant I had kept, who came from Berne, to take care of Le Duc, to put him under good medical superintendence, and to bid the doctor spare nothing to cure him completely.

I dined with my housekeeper in her room, for she had a separate lodging, and after sending my letter to M. de Muralt I went out for a walk.

CHAPTER XVII

Berne—La Mata Madame de la Saone—Sara—My Departure—
Arrival at Bale

I reached an elevation from which I could look over a vast stretch of country watered by a little river, and noticing a path leading to a kind of stair, the fancy took me to follow it. I went down about a hundred steps, and found forty small closets which I concluded were bathing machines. While I was looking at the place an honest-looking fellow came up to me, and asked me if I would like a bath. I said I would, and he opened one of the closets, and before long I surrounded by a crowd of young girls.

"Sir," said the man, "they all aspire to the honour of attending you while you bathe; you have only to choose which it shall be. Half-a-crown will pay for the bath, the girl, and your coffee."

As if I were the Grand Turk, I examined the swarm of rustic beauties, and threw my handkerchief at the one I liked the best. We went into a closet, and shutting the door with the most serious air, without even looking at me, she undressed me, and put a cotton cap on my head, and as soon as she saw me in the water she undressed herself as coolly as possible, and without a word came into the bath. Then she rubbed me all over, except in a certain quarter, which I had covered with my hands. When I thought I had been manipulated sufficiently, I asked for coffee. She got out of the bath, opened the door, and after asking for what I wanted got in again without the slightest consciousness.

When the coffee came she got out again to take it, shut the door, and returned to the bath, and held the tray while I was drinking, and when I had finished she remained beside me.

Although I had taken no great notice of her, I could see that she possessed all the qualifications a man could desire in a woman: fine features, lively eyes, a pretty mouth, and an excellent row of teeth, a healthy complexion, a well-rounded bosom a curved back, and all else in the same sort. I certainly thought her hands might have been softer, but their hardness was probably due to hard work. Furthermore, she was only eighteen, and yet I remained cold to all her charms. How was that? That was the question I asked myself; and I think the reason probably was that she was too natural, too devoid of those assumed graces and coquettish airs which women employ with so much art for the seduction of men. We only care for artifice and false show. Perhaps, too, our senses, to be irritated, require woman's charms to be veiled by modesty. But if, accustomed as we are to clothe ourselves, the face is the smallest factor in our perfect happiness, how is it that the face plays the principal part in rendering a man amorous? Why do we take the face as an index of a woman's beauty, and why do we forgive her when the covered parts are not in harmony with her features? Would it not be much more reasonable and sensible to veil the face, and to have the rest of the body naked? Thus when we fall in love with a woman, we should only want, as the crown of our bliss, to see a face answerable to those other charms which had taken our fancy. There can be no doubt that that would be the better plan, as in that case we should only be seduced by a perfect beauty, and we should grant an easy pardon if at the lifting of the mask we found ugliness instead of loveliness. Under those circumstances an ugly woman, happy in exercising the seductive power of her other charms, would never consent to unveil herself; while the pretty ones would not have to be asked. The plain women would not make us sigh for long; they would be easily subdued on the condition of remaining veiled, and if they did consent to unmask, it would be only after they had practically convinced one that enjoyment is possible without facial beauty. And it is evident and undeniable that inconstancy only proceeds from the variety of features. If a man did not see the face, he would always be constant and always in love with the first woman who had taken his fancy. I know that in the opinion of the foolish all this will seem folly, but I shall not be on the earth to answer their objections.

When I had left the bath, she wiped me with towels, put on my shirt, and then in the same state—that is, quite naked, she did my hair.

While I was dressing she dressed herself too, and having soon finished she came to buckle my shoes. I then gave her half-a-crown for the bath and six francs for herself; she kept the half-crown, but gave me back the six francs with silent contempt. I was mortified; I saw that I had offended her, and that she considered her behaviour entitled her to respect. I went away in a bad enough humour.

After supper I could not help telling my dear Dubois of the adventure I had had in the afternoon, and she made her own comments on the details. "She can't have been pretty," said she, "for if she had been, you would certainly have given way. I should like to see her."

"If you like I will take you there."

"I should be delighted."

"But you will have to dress like a man."

She rose, went out without a word, and in a quarter of an hour returned in a suit of Le Duc's, but minus the trousers, as she had certain protuberances which would have stood out too much I told her to take a pair of my breeches, and we settled to go to the bath next morning.

She came to wake at six o'clock. She was dressed like a man, and wore a blue overcoat which disguised her shape admirably. I rose and went to La Mata, as the place is called.

Animated by the pleasure the expedition gave her, my dear Dubois looked radiant. Those who saw her must have seen through her disguise, she was so evidently a woman; so she wrapped herself up in her overcoat as well as she could.

As soon as we arrived we saw the master of the baths, who asked me if I wanted a closet for four, and I replied in the affirmative. We were soon surrounded by the girls, and I shewed my housekeeper the one who had not seduced me; she made choice of her, and I having fixed upon a big, determined-looking wench, we shut ourselves up in the bath.

As soon as I was undressed I went into the water with my big attendant. My housekeeper was not so quick; the novelty of the thing astonished her, and her expression told me that she repented of having come; but putting a good face on it, she began to laugh at seeing me rubbed by the feminine grenadier. She had some trouble before she could take off her chemise, but as it is only the first step that costs, she let it fall off, and though she held her two hands before her she dazzled me, in spite of myself, by the beauty of her form. Her attendant prepared to treat her as she had treated me, but she begged to be left alone; and on my following her example she felt obliged to let me look after her.

The two Swiss girls, who had no doubt often been present at a similar situation, began to give us a spectacle which was well known to me, but which was quite strange to my dear Dubois.

These two Bacchantes began to imitate the caresses I lavished on my housekeeper, who was quite astonished at the amorous fury with which my attendant played the part of a man with the other girl. I confess I was a little surprised myself, in spite of the transports which my fair Venetian nun had shewn me six years before in conjunction with C—— C——.

I could not have imagined that anything of the kind could have distracted my attention, holding, as I did, the woman I loved, whose charms were sufficient to captivate all the senses; but the strange strife of the two young Menads took up her attention as well as mine.

"Your attendant," said she, "must be a boy, not a girl."

"But," said I, "you saw her breasts."

"Yes, but she may be a boy all the same."

The big Swiss girl who had heard what we had said turned round and shewed me what I should not have credited. There could be no mistake, however. It was a feminine membrane, but much longer than my little finger, and stiff enough to penetrate. I explained to my dear Dubois what it was, but to convince her I had to make her touch it. The impudent creature pushed her shamelessness so far as to offer to try it on her, and she insisted so passionately that I was obliged to push her away. She then turned to her companion and satiated on her body her fury of lust. In spite of its disgusting nature, the sight irritated us to such a degree that my housekeeper yielded to nature and granted me all I could desire.

This entertainment lasted for two hours, and we returned to the town well pleased with one another. On leaving the bath I gave a Louis to each of the two Bacchantes, and we went away determined to go there no more. It will be understood that after what had happened there could be no further obstacle to the free progress of our love; and accordingly my dear Dubois became my mistress, and we made each other happy during all the time we spent at Berne. I was quite cured of my misadventure with the horrible widow, and I found that if love's pleasures are fleeting so are its pains. I will go farther and maintain that the pleasures are of much longer duration, as they leave memories which can be enjoyed in old age, whereas, if a man does happen to remember the pains, it is so slightly as to have no influence upon his happiness.

At ten o'clock the Mayor of Thun was announced. He was dressed in the French fashion, in black, and had a manner at once graceful and polite that pleased me. He was middle-aged, and enjoyed a considerable position in the Government. He insisted on my reading the letter that M. de Chavigni had written to him on my account. It was so flattering that I told him that if it had not been sealed I should not have had the face to deliver it. He asked me for the next day to a supper composed of men only, and for the day after that, to a supper at which women as well as men would be present. I went with him to the library where we saw M. Felix, an unfrocked monk, more of a scribbler than a scholar, and a young man named Schmidt, who gave good promise, and was already known to advantage in the literary world. I also had the misfortune of meeting here a very learned man of a very wearisome kind; he knew the names of ten thousand shells by heart, and I was obliged to listen to him for two hours, although I was totally ignorant of his science. Amongst other things he told me that the Aar contained gold. I replied that all great rivers contained gold, but he shrugged his shoulders and did not seem convinced.

I dined with M. de Muralt in company with four or five of the most distinguished women in Berne. I liked them very well, and above all Madame de Saconai struck me as particularly amiable and well-educated. I should have paid my addresses to her if I had been staying long in the so-called capital of Switzerland.

The ladies of Berne are well though not extravagantly dressed, as luxury is forbidden by the laws. Their manners are good and they speak French with perfect ease. They enjoy the greatest liberty without abusing it, for in spite of gallantry decency reigns everywhere. The husbands are not jealous, but they require their wives to be home by supper-time.

I spent three weeks in the town, my time being divided between my dear Dubois and an old lady of eighty-five who interested me greatly by her knowledge of chemistry. She had been intimately connected with the celebrated Boerhaave, and she shewed me a plate of gold he had transmuted in her presence from copper. I believed as much as I liked of this, but she assured me that Boerhaave possessed the philosopher's stone, but that he had not discovered the secret of prolonging life many years beyond the century. Boerhaave, however, was not able to apply this knowledge to himself, as he died of a polypus on the heart before he had attained the age of perfect maturity, which Hypocrates fixes at between sixty and seventy years. The four millions he left to his daughter, if they do not prove that he could make gold, certainly prove that he could save it. The worthy old woman told me he had given her a manuscript in which the whole process was explained, but that she found it very obscure.

"You should publish it," said I.

"God forbid!"

"Burn it, then."

"I can't make up my mind to do so."

M. de Muralt took me to see the military evolutions gone through by the citizens of Berne, who are all soldiers, and I asked him the meaning of the bear to be seen above the gate of the town. The German for bear is 'bar', 'bern', and the animal has given its name to the town and canton which rank second in the Republic, although it is in the first place for its wealth and culture. It is a peninsula formed by the Aar, which rises near the Rhine. The mayor spoke to me of the power of the canton, its lordships and bailiwicks, and explained his own powers; he then described the public policy, and told me of the different systems of government which compose the Helvetic Union.

"I understand perfectly well," I said, "that each of the thirteen cantons has its own government."

"I daresay you do," he replied, "but what you don't understand any more than I do is, that there is a canton which has four separate governments."

I had an excellent supper with fourteen or fifteen senators. There were no jokes, no frivolous conversation, and no literature; but law, the commonweal, commerce, political economy, speculation, love of country, and the duty of preferring liberty to life, in abundance.

I felt as if I were in a new element, but I enjoyed the privilege of being a man amidst men who were all in honour to our common humanity. But as the supper went on, these rigid republicans began to expand, the discourse became less measured, there were even some bursts of laughter, owing to the wine. I excited their pity, and though they praised sobriety they thought mine excessive. However, they respected my liberty, and did not oblige me to drink, as the Russians, Swedes, Poles, and most northern peoples do.

We parted at midnight—a very late hour in Switzerland, and as they wished me a good night, each of them made me a sincere offer of his friendship. One of the company at an early period of the supper, before he had begun to get mellow, had condemned the Venetian Republic for banishing the Grisons, but on his intellect being enlightened by Bacchus he made his apologies.

"Every government," said he, "ought to know its own interests better than strangers, and everybody should be allowed to do what he wills with his own."

When I got home I found my housekeeper lying in my bed. I gave her a hundred caresses in witness of my joy, and I assured her practically of my love and gratitude. I considered her as my wife, we cherished each other, and did not allow the thought of separating to enter our minds. When two lovers love each other in all freedom, the idea of parting seems impossible.

Next morning I got a letter from the worthy Madame d'Urfe, who begged me to call on Madame de la Saone, wife of a friend of hers—a lieutenant-general. This lady had come to Berne in the hope of getting cured of a disease which had disfigured her in an incredible manner. Madame de la Saone was immediately introduced to all the best society in the place. She gave a supper every day, only asking men; she had an excellent cook. She had given notice that she would pay no calls, and she was quite right.

I hastened to make my bow to her; but, good Heavens! what a terrible and melancholy sight did I behold!

I saw a woman dressed with the utmost elegance, reclining voluptuously upon a couch. As soon as she saw me she arose, gave me a most gracious reception, and going back to her couch invited me to sit beside her. She doubtless noticed my surprise, but being probably accustomed to the impression which the first sight of her created, she talked on in the most friendly manner, and by so doing diminished my aversion.

Her appearance was as follows: Madame de Saone was beautifully dressed, and had the whitest hands and the roundest arms that can be imagined. Her dress, which was cut very low, allowed me to see an exquisite breast of dazzling whiteness, heightened by two rosy buds; her figure was good, and her feet the smallest I have ever seen. All about her inspired love, but when one's eyes turned to her face every other feeling gave way to those of horror and pity. She was fearful. Instead of a face, one saw a blackened and disgusting scab. No feature was distinguishable, and her ugliness was made more conspicuous and dreadful by two fine eyes full of fire, and by a lipless mouth which she kept parted, as if to disclose two rows of teeth of dazzling whiteness. She could not laugh, for the pain caused by the contraction of the muscles would doubtless have drawn tears to her eyes; nevertheless she appeared contented, her conversation was delightful, full of wit and humour, and permeated with the tone of good society. She might be thirty at the most, and she had left three beautiful young children behind in Paris. Her husband was a fine, well-made man, who loved her tenderly, and had never slept apart from her. It is probable that few soldiers have shewn such courage as this, but it is to be supposed that he did not carry his bravery so far as to kiss her, as the very thought made one shudder. A disorder contracted after her first child-bed had left the poor woman in this sad state, and she had borne it for ten years. All the best doctors in France had tried in vain to cure her, and she had come to Berne to put herself into the hands of two well-known physicians who had promised to do so. Every quack makes promises of this sort; their patients are cured or not cured as it happens, and provided that they pay heavily the doctor is ready enough to lay the fault, not on his ignorance, but at the door of his poor deluded patient.

The doctor came while I was with her, and just as her intelligent conversation was making me forget her face. She had already began to take his remedies, which were partly composed of mercury.

"It seems to me," said she, "that the itching has increased since I have taken your medicines."

"It will last," said the son of AEsculapius, "till the end of the cure, and that will take about three months."

"As long as I scratch myself," said she, "I shall be in the same state, and the cure will never be completed."

The doctor replied in an evasive manner. I rose to take my leave, and holding my hand she asked me to supper once for all. I went the same evening; the poor woman took everything and drank some wine, as the doctor had not put her on any diet. I saw that she would never be cured.

Her good temper and her charming conversational powers kept all the company amused. I conceived that it would be possible to get used to her face, and to live with her without being disgusted. In the evening I talked about her to my housekeeper, who said that the beauty of her body and her mental endowments might be sufficient to attract people to her. I agreed, though I felt that I could never become one of her lovers.

Three or four days after, I went to a bookseller's to read the newspaper, and was politely accosted by a fine young man of twenty, who said that Madame de la Saone was sorry not to have seen me again at supper.

"You know the lady?"

"I had the honour to sup at her house with you."

"True; I remember you."

"I get her the books she likes, as I am a bookseller, and not only do I sup with her every evening, but we breakfast together every morning before she gets up."

"I congratulate you. I bet you are in love with her."

"You are pleased to jest, but she is pleasanter than you think."

"I do not jest at all, but I would wager she would not have the courage to push things to an extremity."

"Perhaps you would lose."

"Really? I should be very glad to."

"Let us make a bet."

"How will you convince me I have lost?"

"Let us bet a louis, and you must promise to be discreet."

"Very good."

"Come and sup at her house this evening, and I will tell you something."

"You shall see me there."

When I got home I told my housekeeper what I had heard.

"I am curious to know," said she, "how he will convince you." I promised to tell her, which pleased her very much.

I was exact to my appointment. Madame de la Saone reproached me pleasantly for my absence, and gave me a delicious supper. The young bookseller was there, but as his sweetheart did not speak a word to him he said nothing and passed unnoticed.

After supper we went out together, and he told me on the way that if I liked he would satisfy me the next morning at eight o'clock. "Call here, and the lady's maid will tell you her mistress is not visible, but you have only to say that you will wait, and that you will go into the ante-chamber. This room has a glass door commanding a view of madame's bed, and I will take care to draw back the curtains over the door so that you will be able to see at your ease all that passes between us. When the affair is over I shall go out by another door, she will call her maid, and you will be shewn in. At noon, if you will allow me, I will bring you some books to the 'Falcon,' and if you find that you have lost you shall pay me my louis." I promised to carry out his directions, and we parted.

I was curious to see what would happen, though I by no means regarded it as an impossibility; and on my presenting myself at eight o'clock, the maid let me in as soon as I said that I could wait. I found a corner of the glass door before which there was no curtain, and on applying my eye to the place I saw my young adventurer holding his conquest in his arms on the bed. An enormous nightcap entirely concealed her face—an excellent precaution which favoured the bookseller's enterprise.

When the rascal saw that I had taken up my position, he did not keep me waiting, for, getting up, he presented to my dazzled gaze, not only the secret treasures of his sweetheart, but his own also. He was a small man, but where the lady was most concerned he was a Hercules, and the rogue seemed to make a parade of his proportions as if to excite my jealousy. He turned his victim round so that I should see her under all aspects, and treated her manfully, while she appeared to respond to his ardour with all her might. Phidias could not have modelled his Venus on a finer body; her form was rounded and voluptuous, and as white as Parian marble. I was affected in a lively manner by the spectacle, and re-entered my lodging so inflamed that if my dear Dubois had not been at hand to quench my fire I should have been obliged to have extinguished it in the baths of La Mata.

When I had told her my tale she wanted to know the hero of it, and at noon she had that pleasure. The young bookseller brought me some books I had ordered, and while paying him for them I gave him our bet and a Louis over and above as a mark of my satisfaction at his prowess. He took it with a smile which seemed to shew that he thought I ought to think myself lucky to have lost. My housekeeper looked at him for some time, and asked if he knew her; he said he did not.

"I saw you when you were a child," said she. "You are the son of M. Mignard, minister of the Gospel. You must have been ten when I saw you."

"Possibly, madam."

"You did not care to follow your father's profession, then?"

"No madam, I feel much more inclined to the worship of the creature than to that of the Creator, and I did not think my father's profession would suit me."

"You are right, for a minister of the Gospel ought to be discreet, and discretion is a restraint."

This stroke made him blush, but we did not give him time to lose courage. I asked him to dine with me, and without mentioning the name of Madame de la Saone he told his amorous adventures and numerous anecdotes about the pretty women of Berne.

After he had gone, my housekeeper said that once was quite enough to see a young man of his complexion. I agreed with her, and had no more to do with him; but I heard that Madame de Saone took him to Paris and made his fortune. Many fortunes are made in this manner, and there are some which originated still more nobly. I only returned to Madame de la Saone to take my leave, as I shall shortly relate.

I was happy with my charmer, who told me again and again that with me she lived in bliss. No fears or doubts as to the future troubled her mind; she was certain, as I was, that we should never leave each other; and she told me she would pardon all the infidelities I might be guilty of, provided I made full confession. Hers, indeed, was a disposition with which to live in peace and content, but I was not born to enjoy such happiness.

After we had been a fortnight at Berne, my housekeeper received a letter from Soleure. It came from Lebel. As I saw she read it with great attention, I asked her what it was about.

"Take it and read it," said she; and she sat down in front of me to read my soul by the play of my features.

Lebel asked her, in concise terms, if she would become his wife.

"I have only put off the proposition," said he, "to set my affairs in order, and to see if I could afford to marry you, even if the consent of the ambassador were denied us. I find I am rich enough to live well in Berne or elsewhere without the necessity of my working; however I shall not have to face the alternative, for at the first hint of the matter M. de Chavigni gave his consent with the best grace imaginable."

He went on begging her not to keep him long waiting for a reply, and to tell him in the first place if she consented; in the second, whether she would like to live at Berne and be mistress in her own house, or whether she would prefer to return to Soleure and live with the ambassador, which latter plan might bring them some profit. He ended by declaring that whatever she had would be for her sole use, and that he would give her a dower of a hundred thousand francs. He did not say a word about me.

"Dearest," said I, "you are at perfect liberty to choose your own course, but I cannot contemplate your leaving me without considering myself as the most unhappy of men."

"And if I lose you I should be the most unhappy of women; for if you love me I care not whether we are married or no."

"Very good; but what answer are you going to make."

"You shall see my letter to-morrow. I shall tell him politely but plainly that I love you, that I am yours, that I am happy, and that it is thus impossible for me to accept his flattering propositions. I shall also say that I appreciate his generosity, and that if I were wise I should accept him, but that being the slave of my love for you I can only follow my inclination."

"I think you give an excellent turn to your letter. In refusing such an offer you could not have better reasons than those you give, and it would be absurd to try and persuade him that we are not lovers, as the thing is self-evident. Nevertheless, my darling, the letter saddens me."

"Why, dearest?"

"Because I have not a hundred thousand francs to offer you."

"I despise them; and if you were to offer me such a sum, I should only accept it to lay it at your feet. You are certainly not destined to become miserable, but if that should come to pass, be sure that I should be only too happy to share your misery."

We fell into one another's arms, and love made us taste all its pleasures. Nevertheless, in the midst of bliss, some tinge of sadness gained upon our souls. Languishing love seems to redouble its strength, but it is only in appearance; sadness exhausts love more than enjoyment. Love is a madcap who must be fed on laughter and mirth, otherwise he dies of inanition.

Next day my sweetheart wrote to Lebel in the sense she had decided on, and I felt obliged to write M. de Chavigni a letter in which love, sentiment, and philosophy were mingled. I did not conceal from him that I loved the woman whom Lebel coveted to distraction, but I said that as a man of honour I would rather die than deprive my sweetheart of such solid advantages.

My letter delighted the housekeeper, for she was anxious to know what the ambassador thought of the affair, which needed much reflection.

I got on the same day the letters of introduction I had asked Madame d'Urfe to give me, and I determined, to the joy of my dear Dubois, to set out for Lausanne. But we must hark back a little.

When one is sincerely in love, one thinks the beloved object full of deserts, and the mind, the dupe of the feelings, thinks all the world jealous of its bliss.

A. M. de F——, member of the Council of the Two Hundred, whom I had met at Madame de la Saone's, had become my friend. He came to see me and I introduced him to my dear Dubois, whom he treated with the same distinction he would have used towards my wife. He had presented us to his wife, and had come several times to see us with her and her daughter Sara. Sara was only thirteen, but she was extremely precocious, dark complexioned, and full of wit; she was continually uttering naivetes, of which she understood the whole force, although looking at her face one would have thought her perfectly innocent. She excelled in the art of making her father and mother believe in her innocence, and thus she enjoyed plenty of liberty.

Sara had declared that she was in love with my housekeeper, and as her parents laughed at her she lavished her caresses on my dear Dubois. She often came to breakfast with us, and when she found us in bed she would embrace my sweetheart, whom she called her wife, passing her hand over the coverlet to tickle her, telling her that she was her wife, and that she wanted to have a child. My sweetheart laughed and let her go on.

One day I told her jokingly that she would make me jealous, that I thought she really was a man, and that I was going to make sure.

The sly little puss told me that I was making a mistake, but her hand seemed rather to guide mine than to oppose it. That made me curious, and my mind was soon set at rest as to her sex. Perceiving that she had taken me in and got exactly what she wanted, I drew back my hand, and imparted my suspicions to my housekeeper, who said I was right. However, as the little girl had no part in my affections, I did not push the thing any farther.

Two or three days after, this girl came in as I was getting up, and said in her usual simple way,

"Now that you know I am not really a man you can not be jealous or have objection to my taking your place beside my little wife, if she will let me."

My housekeeper, who looked inclined to laugh, said,

"Come along."

In the twinkling of an eye she was undressed and in the arms of her little wife, whom she proceeded to treat as an amorous husband. My sweetheart laughed, and Sara, having contrived in the combat to rid herself of her chemise and the coverlet, displayed herself to me without any veil, while at the same time she shewed me all the beauties of my sweetheart. This sight inflamed me. I shut the door, and made the little hussy witness of my ardour with my sweetheart. Sara looked on attentively, playing the part of astonishment to perfection, and when I had finished she said, with the utmost simplicity,

"Do it again."

"I can't, my dear; don't you see I am a dead man?"

"That's very funny," she cried; and with the most perfect innocence she came over, and tried to effect my resurrection.

When she had succeeded in placing me in the wished-for condition, she said, "Now go in;" and I should doubtless have obeyed, but my housekeeper said, "No, dearest, since you have effected its resurrection, you must make it die again."

"I should like to," said she, "but I am afraid I have not got enough room;" and so saying she placed herself in a position to shew me that she was speaking the truth, and that if she did not make me die it was not her fault.

Imitating her simplicity I approached her, as if I wished to oblige her, but not to go too far; but not finding any resistance I accomplished the act in all its forms, without her giving the slightest evidence of pain, without any of the accidents of a first trial, but, on the contrary, with all the marks of the utmost enjoyment.

Although I was sure of the contrary, I kept my self-possession enough to tell my housekeeper that Sara had given me what can only be given once, and she pretended to believe me.

When the operation was finished, we had another amusing scene. Sara begged us not to say a word about it to her papa or mamma, as they would be sure to scold her as they had scolded her when she got her ears pierced without asking their leave.

Sara knew that we saw through her feigned simplicity, but she pretended not to do so as it was to her own advantage. Who could have instructed her in the arts of deceit? Nobody; only her natural wit, less rare in childhood than in youth, but always rare and astonishing. Her mother said her simplicities shewed that she would one day be very intelligent, and her father maintained that they were signs of her stupidity. But if Sara had been stupid, our bursts of laughter would have disconcerted her; and she would have died for shame, instead of appearing all the better pleased when her father deplored her stupidity. She would affect astonishment, and by way of curing one sort of stupidity she corroborated it by displaying another. She asked us questions to which we could not reply, and laughed at her instead, although it was evident that before putting such questions she must have reasoned over them. She might have rejoined that the stupidity was on our side, but by so doing she would have betrayed herself.

Lebel did not reply to his sweetheart, but M. de Chavigni wrote me a letter of four pages. He spoke like a philosopher and an experienced man of the world.

He shewed me that if I were an old man like him, and able to insure a happy and independent existence to my sweetheart after my death, I should do well to keep her from all men, especially as there was so perfect a sympathy between us; but that as I was a young man, and did not intend to bind myself to her by the ties of marriage, I should not only consent to a union which seemed for her happiness, but that as a man of honour it was my duty to use my influence with her in favour of the match. "With your experience," said the kind old gentleman, "you ought to know that a time would come when you would regret both having lost this opportunity, for your love is sure to become friendship, and then another love will replace that which you now think as firm as the god Terminus.

"Lebel," he added, "has told me his plans, and far from disapproving, I have encouraged him, for your charming friend won my entire esteem in the five or six times I had the pleasure of seeing her with you. I shall be delighted, therefore, to have her in my house, where I can enjoy her conversation without transgressing the laws of propriety. Nevertheless, you will understand that at my age I have formed no desires, for I could not satisfy them even if their object were propitious." He ended by telling me that Lebel had not fallen in love in a young man's style, that he had reflected on what he was doing, and that he would consequently not hurry her, as she would see in the letter he was going to send her. A marriage ought always to be undertaken in cold blood.

I gave the letter to my housekeeper, who read it attentively, and gave it back to me quite coolly.

"What do you think of his advice, dearest?"

"I think I had better follow it: he says there is no hurry, and delay is all we want. Let us love each other and think only of that. This letter is written with great wisdom, but I cannot imagine our becoming indifferent to each other, though I know such a thing is possible."

"Never indifferent; you make a mistake there."

"Well, friends, then; and that is not much better after being lovers."

"But friendship, dearest, is never indifferent. Love, it is true, may be in its composition. We know it, as it has been thus from the beginning of the world."

"Then the ambassador was right. Repentance might come and torment us when love had been replaced by calmer friendship."

"If you think so, let us marry each other to-morrow, and punish thereby the vices of our human nature."

"Yes, we will marry, but there is no hurry; fearing lest hymen should quicken the departure of love, let us enjoy our happiness while we can."

"You speak admirably, my angel, and deserve the greatest good fortune."

"I wish for no greater than what you procure me."

We went to bed, continuing our discussions, and when we were in each other's arms we made an arrangement which suited us very well.

"Lausanne," said she, "is a little town where you would meet with the warmest hospitality, and during your fortnight's stay you will have nothing to do but to make visits and to go to suppers. I am known to all the nobility, and the Duke of Rosebury, who wearied me with his love-making, is still there. My appearance with you will make everybody talk, and it will be as annoying for you as for me. My mother lives there, too. She would say nothing, but in her heart she would be ill-pleased to see me as the housekeeper of a man like you, for common sense would inform everyone that I was your mistress."

I thought she was right, and that it would be well to respect the rules of society. We decided that she should go to Lausanne by herself and stay with her mother, that in two or three days I should follow her, and should live by myself, as long as I liked, having full liberty to see her at her mother's.

"When you leave Lausanne," said she, "I will rejoin you at Geneva, and then we will travel together where you please and as long as our love lasts."

In two days she started early in the morning, sure of my constancy, and congratulating herself on her discretion. I was sad at her leaving me, but my calls to take leave served to rouse me from my grief. I wished to make M. Haller's acquaintance before I left Switzerland, and the mayor, M. de Muralt, gave me a letter of introduction to him very handsomely expressed. M. de Haller was the bailiff of Roche.

When I called to take leave of Madame de la Saone I found her in bed, and I was obliged to remain by her bedside for a quarter of an hour. She spoke of her disease, and gave the conversation such a turn that she was able with perfect propriety to let me see that the ravages of the disease had not impaired the beauty of her body. The sight convinced me that Mignard had need of less courage than I thought, and I was within an inch of doing her the same service. It was easy enough to look only at her body, and it would have been difficult to behold anything more beautiful.

I know well that prudes and hypocrites, if they ever read these Memoirs, will be scandalized at the poor lady, but in shewing her person so readily she avenged herself on the malady which had disfigured her. Perhaps, too, her goodness of heart and politeness told her what a trial it was to look at her face, and she wished to indemnify the man who disguised his feelings of repugnance by shewing him what gifts nature had given her. I am sure, ladies, that the most prudish—nay, the most virtuous, amongst you, if you were unfortunate enough to be so monstrously deformed in the face, would introduce some fashion which would conceal your ugliness, and display those beauties which custom hides from view. And doubtless Madame de la Saone would have been more chary of her person if she had been able to enchant with her face like you.

The day I left I dined with M—— I——, and was severely taken to task by pretty Sara for having sent her little wife away before me. The reader will see how I met her again at London three years later. Le Duc was still in the doctor's hands, and very weak; but I made him go with me, as I had a good deal of property, and I could not trust it to anybody else.

I left Berne feeling naturally very sad. I had been happy there, and to this day the thought of it is a pleasant one.

I had to consult Dr. Herrenschwand about Madame d'Urfe, so I stopped at Morat, where he lived, and which is only four leagues from Berne. The doctor made me dine with him that I might try the fish of the lake, which I found delicious. I had intended to go on directly after dinner, but I was delayed by a curiosity of which I shall inform the reader.

After I had given the doctor a fee of two Louis for his advice, in writing, on a case of tapeworm, he made me walk with him by the Avanches road, and we went as far as the famous mortuary of Morat.

"This mortuary," said the doctor, "was constructed with part of the bones of the Burgundians, who perished here at the well-known battle lost by Charles the Bold."

The Latin inscription made me laugh.

"This inscription," said I, "contains an insulting jest; it is almost burlesque, for the gravity of an inscription should not allow of laughter."

The doctor, like a patriotic Swiss, would not allow it, but I think it was false shame on his part. The inscription ran as follows, and the impartial reader can judge of its nature:

"Deo. opt. Max. Caroli inclyti et fortisimi Burgundie duds exercitus Muratum obsidens, ab Helvetiis cesus, hoc sui monumentum reliquit anno MCDLXXVI."

Till then I had had a great idea of Morat. Its fame of seven centuries, three sieges sustained and repulsed, all had given me a sublime notion of it; I expected to see something and saw nothing.

"Then Morat has been razed to the ground?" said I to the doctor.

"Not at all, it is as it always has been, or nearly so."

I concluded that a man who wants to be well informed should read first and then correct his knowledge by travel. To know ill is worse than not to know at all, and Montaigne says that we ought to know things well.

But it was the following comic adventure which made me spend the   night   at Morat:

I found at the inn a young maid who spoke a sort of rustic Italian. She struck me by her great likeness to my fair stocking-seller at Paris. She was called Raton, a name which my memory has happily preserved. I offered her six francs for her favours, but she refused the money with a sort of pride, telling me that I had made a mistake and that she was an honest girl.

"It may be so," said I, and I ordered my horses to be put in. When the honest Raton saw me on the point of leaving, she said, with an air that was at once gay and timid, that she wanted two louis, and if I liked to give her them and pass the night with her I should be well content.

"I will stay, but remember to be kind."

"I will."

When everybody had gone to bed, she came into my room with a little frightened manner, calculated to redouble my ardour, but by great good luck, feeling I had a necessity, I took the light and ran to the place where I could satisfy it. While there I amused myself by reading innumerable follies one finds written in such places, and suddenly my eyes lighted on these words:—

"This tenth day of August, 1760, the wretched Raton gave me the what-d'-you-call-it: reader, beware."

I was almost tempted to believe in miracles, for I could not think there were two Ratons in the same house. I returned gaily to my room and found my sweetheart in bed without her chemise. I went to the place beside the bed where she had thrown it down, and as soon as she saw me touching it she begged me in a fright not to do so, as it was not clean. She was right, for it bore numerous marks of the disease which infected her. It may be imagined that my passion cooled, and that I sent her away in a moment; but I felt at the same time the greatest gratitude to what is called chance, for I should have never thought of examining a girl whose face was all lilies and roses, and who could not be more than eighteen.

Next day I went to Roche to see the celebrated Haller.

CHAPTER XVIII

M. Haller—My Stay at Lausanne—Lord Rosebury—The Young Saconaï—Dissertation on Beauty—The Young Theologian

M. Haller was a man six feet high and broad in a proportion; he was a well-made man, and a physical as well as a mental colossus. He received me courteously, and when he had read M. de Muralt's letter, he displayed the greatest politeness, which shews that a good letter of introduction is never out of place. This learned man displayed to me all the treasures of his knowledge, replying with exactitude to all my questions, and above all with a rare modesty which astonished me greatly, for whilst he explained the most difficult questions, he had the air of a scholar who would fain know; but on the other hand, when he asked me a scientific question, it was with so delicate an art that I could not help giving the right answer.

M. de Haller was a great physiologist, a great doctor, and a great anatomist. He called Morgagni his master, though he had himself made numerous discoveries relating to the frame of man. While I stayed with him he shewed me a number of letters from Morgagni and Pontedera, a professor of botany, a science of which Haller had an extensive knowledge. Hearing me speak of these learned men whose works I had read at an early age, he complained that Pontedera's letters were almost illegible and written in extremely obscure Latin. He shewed me a letter from a Berlin Academician, whose name I have forgotten, who said that since the king had read his letter he had no more thoughts of suppressing the Latin language. Haller had written to Frederick the Great that a monarch who succeeded in the unhappy enterprise of proscribing the language of Cicero and Virgil from the republic of letters would raise a deathless monument to his own ignorance. If men of letters require a universal language to communicate with one another, Latin is certainly the best, for Greek and Arabic do not adapt themselves in the same way to the genius of modern civilization.

Haller was a good poet of the Pindaric kind; he was also an excellent statesman, and had rendered great services to his country. His morals were irreproachable, and I remember his telling me that the only way to give precepts was to do so by example. As a good citizen he was an admirable paterfamilias, for what greater proof could he give of his love of country than by presenting it with worthy subjects in his children, and such subjects result from a good education. His wife was still young, and bore on her features the marks of good nature and discretion. He had a charming daughter of about eighteen; her appearance was modest, and at table she only opened her mouth to speak in a low tone to a young man who sat beside her. After dinner, finding myself alone with M. Haller, I asked him who this young man was. He told me he was his daughter's tutor.

"A tutor like that and so pretty a pupil might easily become lovers."

"Yes, please God."

This Socratic reply made me see how misplaced my remark had been, and I felt some confusion. Finding a book to my hand I opened it to restore my composure.

It was an octavo volume of his works, and I read in it:

"Utrum memoria post mortem dubito."

"You do not think, then," said I, "that the memory is an essential part of the soul?"

"How is that question to be answered?" M. de Haller replied, cautiously, as he had his reasons for being considered orthodox.

During dinner I asked if M. de Voltaire came often to see him. By way of reply he repeated these lines of the poet:—

"Vetabo qui Cereris sacrum vulgarit arcanum sub usdem sit trabibus."

I spent three days with this celebrated man, but I thought myself obliged to refrain from asking his opinion on any religious questions, although I had a great desire to do so, as it would have pleased me to have had his opinion on that delicate subject; but I believe that in matters of that kind M. Haller judged only by his heart. I told him, however, that I should consider a visit to Voltaire as a great event, and he said I was right. He added, without the slightest bitterness,

"M. de Voltaire is a man who ought to be known, although, in spite of the laws of nature, many persons have found him greater at a distance than close at hand."

M. de Haller kept a good and abundant though plain table; he only drank water. At dessert only he allowed himself a small glass of liqueur drowned in an enormous glass of water. He talked a great deal of Boerhaave, whose favourite pupil he had been. He said that after Hypocrates, Boerhaave was the greatest doctor and the greatest chemist that had ever existed.

"How is it," said I, "that he did not attain mature age?"

"Because there is no cure for death. Boerhaave was born a doctor, as Homer was born a poet; otherwise he would have succumbed at the age of fourteen to a malignant ulcer which had resisted all the best treatment of the day. He cured it himself by rubbing it constantly with salt dissolved in his own urine."

"I have been told that he possessed the philosopher's stone."

"Yes, but I don't believe it."

"Do you think it possible?"

"I have been working for the last thirty years to convince myself of its impossibility; I have not yet done so, but I am sure that no one who does not believe in the possibility of the great work can be a good chemist."

When I left him he begged me to write and tell him what I thought of the great Voltaire, and in, this way our French correspondence began. I possess twenty-two letters from this justly celebrated man; and the last word written six months before, his too, early death. The longer I live the more interest I take in my papers. They are the treasure which attaches me to life and makes death more hateful still.

I had been reading at Berne Rousseau's "Heloïse," and I asked M. Haller's opinion of it. He told me that he had once read part of it to oblige a friend, and from this part he could judge of the whole. "It is the worst of all romances, because it is the most eloquently expressed. You will see the country of Vaud, but don't expect to see the originals of the brilliant portraits which Jean Jacques painted. He seems to have thought that lying was allowable in a romance, but he has abused the privilege. Petrarch, was a learned man, and told no lies in speaking of his love for Laura, whom he loved as every man loves the woman with whom he is taken; and if Laura had not contented her illustrious lover, he would not have celebrated her."

Thus Haller spoke to me of Petrarch, mentioning Rousseau with aversion. He disliked his very eloquence, as he said it owed all its merits to antithesis and paradox. Haller was a learned man of the first class, but his knowledge was not employed for the purpose of ostentation, nor in private life, nor when he was in the company of people who did not care for science. No one knew better than he how to accommodate himself to his company he was friendly with everyone, and never gave offence. But what were his qualifications? It would be much easier to say what he had not than what he had. He had no pride, self-sufficiency, nor tone of superiority—in fact, none of those defects which are often the reproach of the learned and the witty.

He was a man of austere virtue, but he took care to hide the austerity under a veil of a real and universal kindness. Undoubtedly he thought little of the ignorant, who talk about everything right or wrong, instead of remaining silent, and have at bottom only contempt for the learned; but he only shewed his contempt by saying nothing. He knew that a despised ignoramus becomes an enemy, and Haller wished to be loved. He neither boasted of nor concealed his knowledge, but let it run like a limpid stream flowing through the meadows. He talked well, but never absorbed the conversation. He never spoke of his works; when someone mentioned them he would turn the conversation as soon as he conveniently could. He was sorry to be obliged to contradict anyone who conversed with him.

When I reached Lausanne I found myself enabled to retain my incognito for a day at any rate. I naturally gave the first place to my affections. I went straight to my sweetheart without needing to ask my way, so well had she indicated the streets through which I had to pass. I found her with her mother, but I was not a little astonished to see Lebel there also. However, my surprise must have passed unnoticed, for my housekeeper, rising from her seat with a cry of joy, threw her arms about my neck, and after having kissed me affectionately presented me to her worthy mother, who welcomed me in the friendliest manner. I asked Lebel after the ambassador, and how long he had been at Lausanne.

He replied, with a polite and respectful air, that his master was quite well, and that he had come to Lausanne on business, and had only been there a few hours; and that, wishing to pay his regards to Madame Dubois's mother, he had been pleasantly surprised to see the daughter there as well.

"You know," he added, "what my intentions are. I have to go back to-morrow, and when you have made up your minds, write to me and I will come and take her to Soleure, where I will marry her."

He could not have spoken more plainly or honourably. I said that I would never oppose the will of my sweetheart, and my Dubois, interrupting me, said in her turn that she would never leave me until I sent her away.

Lebel found these replies too vague, and told me with noble freedom that we must give him a definite reply, since in such cases uncertainty spoils all. At that moment I felt as if I could never agree to his wishes, and I told him that in ten days I would let him know of our resolution, whatever it was. At that he was satisfied, and left us.

After his departure my sweetheart's mother, whose good sense stood her instead of wit, talked to us in a manner that answered our inclinations, for, amorous as we were, we could not bear the idea of parting. I agreed that my housekeeper should wait up for me till midnight, and that we could talk over our reply with our heads on the pillow.

My Dubois had a separate room with a good bed and excellent furniture. She gave me a very good supper, and we spent a delicious night. In the morning we felt more in love than ever, and were not at all disposed to comply with Lebel's wishes. Nevertheless, we had a serious conversation.

The reader will remember that my mistress had promised to pardon my infidelities, provided that I confessed them. I had none to confess, but in the course of conversation I told her about Raton.

"We ought to think ourselves very fortunate," said she, "for if it had not been for chance, we should have been in a fine state now."

"Yes, and I should be in despair."

"I don't doubt it, and you would be all the more wretched as I should never complain to you."

"I only see one way of providing against such a misfortune. When I have been unfaithful to you I will punish myself by depriving myself of the pleasure of giving you proofs of my affection till I am certain that I can do so without danger."

"Ah! you would punish me for your faults, would you? If you love me as I love you, believe me you would find a better remedy than that."

"What is that?"

"You would never be unfaithful to me."

"You are right. I am sorry I was not the first to think of this plan, which I promise to follow for the future."

"Don't make any promises," said she, with a sigh, "it might prove too difficult to keep them."

It is only love which can inspire such conversations, but unfortunately it gains nothing by them.

Next morning, just as I was going out to take my letters, the Baron   de Bercei, uncle of my friend Bavois, entered.

"I know," said he, "that my nephew owes his fortune to you; he is just going to be made general, and I and all the family will be enchanted to make your acquaintance. I have come to offer my services, and to beg that you will dine with me to-day, and on any other day you please when you have nothing better to do, and I hope you will always consider yourself of the family.

"At the same time I beg of you not to tell anybody that my nephew has become a Catholic, as according to the prejudices of the country it would be a dishonour which would reflect on the whole family."

I accepted his invitation, and promised to say nothing about the circumstance he had mentioned.

I left my letters of introduction, and I received everywhere a welcome of the most distinguished kind. Madame de Gentil-Langalerie appeared the most amiable of all the ladies I called on, but I had not time to pay my court to one more than another. Every day politeness called me to some dinner, supper, ball, or assembly. I was bored beyond measure, and I felt inclined to say how troublesome it is to have such a welcome. I spent a fortnight in the little town, where everyone prides himself on his liberty, and in all my life I have never experienced such a slavery, for I had not a moment to myself. I was only able to pass one night with my sweetheart, and I longed to set off with her for Geneva. Everybody would give me letters of introduction for M. de Voltaire, and by their eagerness one would have thought the great man beloved, whereas all detested him on account of his sarcastic humour.

"What, ladies!" said I, "is not M. de Voltaire good-natured, polite, and affable to you who have been kind enough to act in his plays with him?"

"Not in the least. When he hears us rehearse he grumbles all the time. We never say a thing to please him: here it is a bad pronunciation, there a tone not sufficiently passionate, sometimes one speaks too softly, sometimes too loudly; and it's worse when we are acting. What a hubbub there is if one add a syllable, or if some carelessness spoil one of his verses. He frightens us. So and so laughed badly; so and so in Alzire had only pretended to weep."

"Does he want you to weep really?"

"Certainly. He will have real tears. He says that if an actor wants to draw tears he must shed them himself."

"I think he is right there; but he should not be so severe with amateurs, above all with charming actresses like you. Such perfection is only to be looked for from professionals, but all authors are the same. They never think that the actor has pronounced the words with the force which the sense, as they see it, requires."

"I told him, one day, that it was not my fault if his lines had not the proper force."

"I am sure he laughed."

"Laughed? No, sneered, for he is a rude and impertinent man."

"But I suppose you overlook all these failings?"

"Not at all; we have sent him about his business."

"Sent him about his business?"

"Yes. He left the house he had rented here, at short notice, and retired to where you will find him now. He never comes to see us now, even if we ask him."

"Oh, you do ask him, though you sent him about his business?"

"We cannot deprive ourselves of the pleasure of admiring his talents, and if we have teased him, that was only from revenge, and to teach him something of the manners of good society."

"You have given a lesson to a great master."

"Yes; but when you see him mention Lausanne, and see what he will say of us. But he will say it laughingly, that's his way."

During my stay I often saw Lord Rosebury, who had vainly courted my charming Dubois. I have never known a young man more disposed to silence. I have been told that he had wit, that he was well educated, and even in high spirits at times, but he could not get over his shyness, which gave him an almost indefinable air of stupidity. At balls, assemblies—in fact, everywhere, his manners consisted of innumerable bows. When one spoke to him, he replied in good French but with the fewest possible words, and his shy manner shewed that every question was a trouble to him.

One day when I was dining with him, I asked him some question about his country, which required five or six small phrases by way of answer. He gave me an excellent reply, but blushed all the time like a young girl when she comes out. The celebrated Fox who was then twenty, and was at the same dinner, succeeded in making him laugh, but it was by saying something in English, which I did not understand in the least. Eight months after I saw him again at Turin, he was then amorous of a banker's wife, who was able to untie his tongue.

At Lausanne I saw a young girl of eleven or twelve by whose beauty I was exceedingly struck. She was the daughter of Madame de Saconai, whom I had known at Berne. I do not know her after history, but the impression she made on me has never been effaced. Nothing in nature has ever exercised such a powerful influence over me as a pretty face, even if it be a child's.

The Beautiful, as I have been told, is endowed with this power of attraction; and I would fain believe it, since that which attracts me is necessarily beautiful in my eyes, but is it so in reality? I doubt it, as that which has influenced me has not influenced others. The universal or perfect beauty does not exist, or it does not possess this power. All who have discussed the subject have hesitated to pronounce upon it, which they would not have done if they had kept to the idea of form. According to my ideas, beauty is only form, for that which is not beautiful is that which has no form, and the deformed is the opposite of the 'pulchrum' and 'formosum'.

We are right to seek for the definitions of things, but when we have them to hand in the words; why should we go farther? If the word 'forma' is Latin, we should seek for the Latin meaning and not the French, which, however, often uses 'deforme' or 'difforme' instead of 'laid', ugly, without people's noticing that its opposite should be a word which implies the existence of form; and this can only be beauty. We should note that 'informe' in French as well as in Latin means shapeless, a body without any definite appearance.

We will conclude, then, that it is the beauty of woman which has always exercised an irresistible sway over me, and more especially that beauty which resides in the face. It is there the power lies, and so true is that, that the sphinxes of Rome and Versailles almost make me fall in love with them though, the face excepted, they are deformed in every sense of the word. In looking at the fine proportions of their faces one forgets their deformed bodies. What, then, is beauty? We know not; and when we attempt to define it or to enumerate its qualities we become like Socrates, we hesitate. The only thing that our minds can seize is the effect produced by it, and that which charms, ravishes, and makes me in love, I call beauty. It is something that can be seen with the eyes, and for my eyes I speak. If they had a voice they would speak better than I, but probably in the same sense.

No painter has surpassed Raphael in the beauty of the figures which his divine pencil produced; but if this great painter had been asked what beauty was, he would probably have replied that he could not say, that he knew it by heart, and that he thought he had reproduced it whenever he had seen it, but that he did not know in what it consisted.

"That face pleases me," he would say, "it is therefore beautiful!"

He ought to have thanked God for having given him such an exquisite eye for the beautiful; but 'omne pulchrum difficile'.

The painters of high renown, all those whose works proclaim genius, have excelled in the delineation of the beautiful; but how small is their number compared to the vast craved who have strained every nerve to depict beauty and have only left us mediocrity!

If a painter could be dispensed from making his works beautiful, every man might be an artist; for nothing is easier than to fashion ugliness, and brush and canvas would be as easy to handle as mortar and trowel.

Although portrait-painting is the most important branch of the art, it is to be noted that those who have succeeded in this line are very few. There are three kinds of portraits: ugly likenesses, perfect likenesses, and those which to a perfect likeness add an almost imperceptible character of beauty. The first class is worthy only of contempt and their authors of stoning, for to want of taste and talent they add impertinence, and yet never seem to see their failings. The second class cannot be denied to possess real merit; but the palm belongs to the third, which, unfortunately, are seldom found, and whose authors deserve the large fortunes they amass. Such was the famous Notier, whom I knew in Paris in the year 1750. This great artist was then eighty, and in spite of his great age his talents seemed in all their freshness. He painted a plain woman; it was a speaking likeness, and in spite of that those who only saw the portrait pronounced her to be a handsome woman. Nevertheless, the most minute examination would not have revealed any faithlessness to the original, but some imperceptible touches gave a real but indefinite air of beauty to the whole. Whence does that magic art take its source? One day, when he had been painting the plain-looking "Mesdames de France," who on the canvas looked like two Aspasias, I asked him the above question. He answered:—

"It is a magic which the god of taste distils from my brains through my brushes. It is the divinity of Beauty whom all the world adores, and which no one can define, since no one knows of what it consists. That canvas shews you what a delicate shade there is between beauty and ugliness; and nevertheless this shade seems an enormous difference to those unacquainted with art."

The Greek painters made Venus, the goddess of beauty, squint-eyed, and this odd idea has been praised by some; but these painters were certainly in the wrong.

Two squinting eyes might be beautiful, but certainly not so beautiful as if they did not squint, for whatever beauty they had could not proceed from their deformity.

After this long digression, with which the reader may not be very well pleased, it is time for me to return to my sweetheart. The tenth day of my visit to Lausanne, I went to sup and sleep with my mistress, and that night was the happiest I remember. In the morning, while we were taking coffee with her mother, I observed that we seemed in no hurry to part. At this, the mother, a woman of few words, took up the discourse in a polite and dignified manner, and told me it was my duty to undeceive Lebel before I left; and at the same time she gave me a letter she had had from him the evening before. The worthy man begged her to remind me that if I could not make up my mind to separate from her daughter before I left Lausanne, it would be much more difficult for me to do so when I was farther off; above all, if, as would probably be the case, she gave me a living pledge of her love. He said that he had no thoughts of drawing back from his word, but he should wish to be able to say that he had taken his wife from her mother's hands.

When I had read the letter aloud, the worthy mother wept, and left us alone. A moment's silence ensued, and with a sigh that shewed what it cost her, my dear Dubois had the courage to tell me that I must instantly write to Lebel to give up all pretensions to her, or to come and take her at once.

"If I write and tell him to think no more of you, I must marry you myself."

"No."

With this no she arose and left me. I thought it over for a quarter of an hour, I weighed the pros and cons and still my love shrank from the sacrifice. At last, on consideration that my housekeeper would never have such a chance again, that I was not sure that I could always make her happy, I resolved to be generous, and determined to write to Lebel that Madame Dubois had decided of her own free will to become his wife, that I had no right to oppose her resolution, and that I would go so far as to congratulate him on a happiness I envied him. I begged him to leave Soleure at once and come and receive her in my presence from the hands of her worthy mother.

I signed the letter and took it to my housekeeper, who was in her mother's room. "Take this letter, dearest, and read it, and if you approve its contents put your signature beside mine." She read it several times, while her good mother wept, and then, with an affectionate and sorrowful air, she took the pen and signed. I begged her mother to find somebody to take the letter to Soleure immediately, before my resolution was weakened by repentance.

The messenger came, and as soon as he had gone, "Farewell," said I, embracing her, with my eyes wet with tears, "farewell, we shall see each other again as soon as Lebel comes."

I went to my inn, a prey to the deepest grief. This sacrifice had given a new impetus to my love for this charming woman, and I felt a sort of spasm, which made me afraid I should get ill. I shut myself up in my room, and I ordered the servants to say I was unwell and could see no one.

In the evening of the fourth day after, Lebel was announced. He embraced me, saying his happiness would be due to me. He then left me, telling me he would expect me at the house of his future bride.

"Excuse me to-day, my dear fellow," said I, "but I will dine with you there to-morrow."

When he had left me, I told Le Duc to make all preparations for our leaving the next day after dinner.

I went out early on the following day to take leave of everybody, and at noon Lebel came to take me to that sad repast, at which, however, I was not so sad as I had feared.

As I was leaving I begged the future Madame Lebel to return me the ring I had given her, and as we had agreed, I presented her with a roll of a hundred Louis, which she took with a melancholy air.

"I should never have sold it," she said, "for I have no need of money."

"In that case I will give it back to you, but promise me never to part with it, and keep the hundred Louis as some small reward of the services you have rendered me."

She shook my hand affectionately, put on my finger her wedding ring, and left me to hide her grief. I wiped my tears away, and said to Lebel,

"You are about to possess yourself of a treasure which I cannot commend too highly. You are a man of honour; you will appreciate her excellent qualities, and you will know how to make her happy. She will love you only, take care of your household, and keep no secrets from you. She is full of wit and spirits, and will easily disperse the slightest shadow of ill humour which may fall on you."

I went in with him to the mother's room to take leave of her, and Madame Dubois begged me to delay my departure and sup once more with her. I told her that my horses were put in and the carriage waiting at my door, and that such a delay would set tongues talking; but that if she liked, she, her future husband and her mother, could come and see me at an inn two leagues off on the Geneva road, where we could stay as long as we liked. Lebel approved of the plan, and my proposition was accepted.

When I got back to my inn I found my carriage ready, and I got in and drove to the meeting-place, and ordered a good supper for four, and an hour later my guests arrived.

The gay and even happy air of the newly betrothed surprised me, but what astonished me more was the easy way with which she threw herself into my arms as soon as she saw me. It put me quite out of countenance, but she had more wit than I. However, I mustered up sufficient strength to follow her cue, but I could not help thinking that if she had really loved me she would not have found it possible to pass thus from love to mere friendship. However, I imitated her, and made no objections to those marks of affection allowed to friendship, which are supposed to have no tincture of love in them.

At supper I thought I saw that Lebel was more delighted at having such a wife than at the prospect of enjoying her and satisfying a strong passion. That calmed me; I could not be jealous of a man like that. I perceived, too, that my sweetheart's high spirits were more feigned than real; she wished to make me share them so as to render our separation less bitter, and to tranquillise her future husband as to the nature of our feelings for one another. And when reason and time had quieted the tempest in my heart, I could not help thinking it very natural that she should be pleased at the prospect of being independent, and of enjoying a fortune.

We made an excellent supper, which we washed down so well that at last the gaiety which had been simulated ended by being real. I looked at the charming Dubois with pleasure; I regarded her as a treasure which had belonged to me, and which after making me happy was with my full consent about to ensure the happiness of another. It seemed to me that I had been magnanimous enough to give her the reward she deserved, like a good Mussulman who gives a favourite slave his freedom in return for his fidelity. Her sallies made me laugh and recalled the happy moments I had passed with her, but the idea of her happiness prevented my regretting having yielded my rights to another.

As Lebel was obliged to return to Lausanne in order to get back to Soleure in two days, we had to part. I embraced him and asked him to continue his friendship towards me, and he promised with great effusion to be my friend till death. As we were going down the stair, my charming friend said, with great candour,

"I am not really gay, but I oblige myself to appear so. I shall not be happy till the scar on my heart has healed. Lebel can only claim my esteem, but I shall be his alone though my love be all for you. When we see each other again, as from what you say I hope we shall, we shall be able to meet as true friends, and perhaps we shall congratulate each other on the wise part we have taken. As for you, though I do not think you will forget me, I am sure that before long some more or less worthy object will replace me and banish your sorrow. I hope it will be so. Be happy. I may be with child; and if it prove to be so, you shall have no cause to complain of my care of your child, which you shall take away when you please. We made an agreement on this point yesterday. We arranged that the marriage should not be consummated for two months; thus we shall be certain whether the child belongs to you or no, and we will let people think that it is the legitimate offspring of our marriage. Lebel conceived this plan that he might have his mind at rest on the supposed force of blood, in which he declares he believes no more than I do. He has promised to love the child as if he were its father. If you write to me, I will keep you acquainted with everything; and if I have the happiness to give you a child, it will be much dearer to me than your ring."

We wept, and Lebel laughed to see us.

I could only reply by pressing her to my breast, and then I gave her over to her future husband, who told me as he got into the carriage that our long talk had pleased him very much.

I went to bed sadly enough. Next morning when I awoke, a pastor of the Church of Geneva came to ask me to give him a place in my carriage. I agreed, and was not sorry I had done so.

This priest was an eloquent man, although a theologian, who answered the most difficult religious questions I could put to him. There was no mystery with him, everything was reason. I have never found a more compliant Christianity than that of this worthy man, whose morals, as I heard afterwards at Geneva, were perfectly pure. But I found out that this kind of Christianity was not peculiar to him, all his fellow-Calvinists thought in the same way.

Wishing to convince him that he was a Calvinist in name only, since he did not believe that Jesus Christ was of the same substance as the Father, he replied that Calvin was only infallible where he spoke 'ex cathedra', but I struck him dumb by quoting the words of the Gospel. He blushed when I reproached him with Calvin's belief that the Pope was the Antichrist of the Apocalypse.

"It will be impossible to destroy this prejudice at Geneva," said he, "till the Government orders the effacement of an inscription on the church door which everybody reads, and which speaks of the head of the Roman Church in this manner."

"The people," he added, "are wholly ignorant; but I have a niece of twenty, who does not belong to the people in this way. I shall have the honour of making you known to her; she is a theologian, and pretty as well."

"I shall be delighted to see her, but God preserve me from arguing with her!"

"She will make you argue, and I can assure you that it will be a pleasure for you!"

"We shall see; but will you give me your address?"

"No sir, but I shall have the honour of conducting you to your inn and acting as your guide."

I got down at Balances, and was well lodged. It was the 20th of August, 1760. On going to the window I noticed a pane of glass on which I read these words, written with the point of a diamond: "You will forget Henriette." In a moment my thoughts flew back to the time in which Henriette had written these words, thirteen years ago, and my hair stood on end. We had been lodged in this room when she separated from me to return to France. I was overwhelmed, and fell on a chair where I abandoned myself to deep thought. Noble Henriette, dear Henriette, whom I had loved so well; where was she now? I had never heard of her; I had never asked anyone about her. Comparing my present and past estates, I was obliged to confess that I was less worthy of possessing her now than then. I could still love, but I was no longer so delicate in my thoughts; I had not those feelings which justify the faults committed by the senses, nor that probity which serves as a contrast to the follies and frailties of man; but, what was worst of all, I was not so strong. Nevertheless, it seemed that the remembrance of Henriette restored me to my pristine vigour. I had no longer my housekeeper; I experienced a great void; and I felt so enthusiastic that if I had known where Henriette was I should have gone to seek her out, despite her prohibition.

Next day, at an early hour, I went to the banker Tronchin, who had all my money. After seeing my account, he gave me a letter of credit on Marseilles, Genoa, Florence and Rome, and I only took twelve thousand francs in cash. I had only fifty thousand crowns, three hundred francs, but that would take me a good way. As soon as I had delivered my letters, I returned to Balances, impatient to see M. de Voltaire.

I found my fellow-traveller in my room. He asked me to dinner, telling me that I should have M. Vilars-Chandieu, who would take me after dinner to M. de Voltaire, who had been expecting me for several days. I followed the worthy man, and found at his house excellent company, and the young theologian whom the uncle did not address till dessert.

I will endeavour to report as faithfully as possible the young woman's conversation.

"What have you been doing this morning, my dear niece?"

"I have been reading St. Augustine, whom I thought absurd, and I think I can refute him very shortly."

"On what point?"

"Concerning the mother of the Saviour."

"What does St. Augustine say?"

"You have no doubt remarked the passage, uncle. He says that the Virgin
Mary conceived Jesus Christ through the ears."

"You do not believe that?"

"Certainly not, and for three good reasons. In the first place because God, being immaterial, had no need of a hole to go in or come out by; in the second place, because the ear has no connection with the womb; and in the third place, because Mary, if she had conceived by the ear, would have given birth by the same channel.

This would do well enough for the Catholics," said she, giving me a glance, "as then they would be reasonable in calling her a virgin before her conception, during her pregnancy, and after she had given birth to the child."

I was extremely astonished, and my astonishment was shared by the other guests. Divine theology rises above all fleshly considerations, and after what we had heard we had either to allow her this privilege, or to consider the young theologian as a woman without shame. The learned niece did not seem to care what we thought, as she asked for my opinion on the matter.

"If I were a theologian and allowed myself an exact examination into the miracles, it is possible I should be of your opinion; but as this is by no means the case, I must limit myself to condemning St. Augustine for having analysed the mystery of the Annunciation. I may say, however, that if the Virgin had been deaf, St. Augustine would have been guilty of a manifest absurdity, since the Incarnation would have been an impossibility, as in that case the nerves of the ear would have had no sort of communication with the womb, and the process would have been inconceivable; but the Incarnation is a miracle."

She replied with great politeness that I had shown myself a greater theologian than she, and her uncle thanked me for having given her a lesson. He made her discuss various subjects, but she did not shine. Her only subject was the New Testament. I shall have occasion to speak of this young woman when I get back to Geneva.

After dinner we went to see Voltaire, who was just leaving the table as we came in. He was in the middle of a court of gentlemen and ladies, which made my introduction a solemn one; but with this great man solemnity could not fail to be in my favour.

The End